For Kathryn

Hope you find my book
a Amusing 🙂

Lol   Peter - (30.07.13.)

Tales
of a
Dagenham 'Dustbin Lid'

MY AUTOBIOGRATHY
The Early Years – Red Ryder

1 Red

www.fast-print.net/store.php

TALES OF A DAGENHAM 'DUSTBIN LID'
Copyright © Red Ryder 2013

A catalogue record for this book is available from the British Library

ISBN 978-178035-661-7

First published 2013 by
FASTPRINT PUBLISHING
Peterborough, England.

In Loving memory of

My Parents, Grandma Baylis, Maggi and Donald

My Dear Great Nephew - Gary

And

To Iris for our Kiwi/Cockney chats

Foreword

I have tried to put together in this book my experiences of a boy set in the 50s' from about 1950 to 1960. Incidences, that happened to me and stupid things that I did during that period.

I always regret that my parents, as they grew older never described in detail what their lives were like, especially as they experienced the hard years of the 1930s, and the Second World War. My Father-in-Law also had great memories as he manned the gun Lights in the war both in Belgium and at home, but never put his memories in to print.

Obviously I have never experienced such hardships as my parents' generation, but at least in this book of memories and photos I can leave some form of legacy if not of interest to the public then at least to my grandchildren who may find this of some interest with a few smiles thrown in for good measure, although I am sure my oldest, 'Megan' has heard most of these stories already

From the age of five (1950) through to the age of fifteen are the years I have concentrated on, although I might cheat a little bit and extend it to 1963.

When reading my exploits in this book the reader should also be aware of my illness to asthma attacks, extreme shyness and insecurities brought on by the unsettling home life that I unknowingly endured which may or may not explain some of my actions. Also I am a 'ginger-nut' a most affectionate term for them days or ginger to my mates and enemies alike.

I came in to this world on the 11th June 1945 on the Rylands' estate in Dagenham, Third Avenue, a stones throw away from the ABC Cinema at the Princes road. Where many of my early exploits began, the fourth in line to my parents' three bedroom terrace house. Ma and Pa were actually buying their house, which was an unheard thing at that time for working class folk.

I shared an eight by six foot bedroom with my brother, seven years older than me and a *'bloody pain'*. My two sisters shared the other room they were 10 and 11 years older than me and that room was even smaller. My Father was the only child of strict parents but he was educated and qualified as a mechanical engineer, spending most of my life as I knew it, working 'shift' work at the Ford foundry. Finally my Mother who was one of eight children, six boys and one sister, probably got my hair colouring from her..............or the milkman as my brother would say!

To the uninitiated a *'Dustbin Lid'* is cockney rhyming slang for a 'kid'

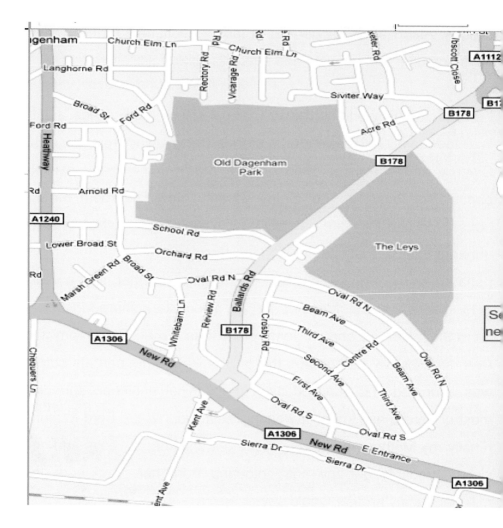

Ryland's Estate

Episode 1 – Earliest Memories

"Jimmy, go and get the horse while I climb this tree and don't be to long about it?

 The farmer will be after us and I don't want to be stuck up here while you run away……alright Ginger, won't be a second"

But he was about fifteen minutes chasing this bloody horse around the field until finally he got hold of the rope that was tied to the neck of the Mayor. I was about fifteen feet up an old oak tree, hanging out on a branch ready to drop onto this old cart- horse.

It was a wonderful sunny spring day, no one about. Me and Jimmy were just looking for an adventure. We were 5 to 6 year olds at the time. Hard to believe that my mother would let me out so young. She didn't! I would always run out of the house when she wasn't looking and she would always give me a 'telling off' and a 'whack' when I returned – but it never bothered me……….hard as nails, me.

"OK Jimmy hold the rope tight, here I come" 'whoosh'….. as I jumped down on to the horse's back, it reared up but I hung on to its mane as jimmy let go, we bolted off over the field until it calmed down, it must have taken about ten minutes until it finally realised I wasn't going to harm him.

Anyway I managed to kick its belly with my small legs and got it back to the same tree again. This time Jimmy was up the tree and he leaped but the horse moved…………………..he fell straight down to the ground.

The horse bolted again, I fell off, Jimmy broke his arm the farmer headed straight for us from where, I don't know. Jimmy got up and we ran as fast as we could, calling the farmer names as we fled. What fun we had!

Jimmy lived in the same street as me *'Third Avenue'* I didn, t see him again for about three weeks. He told his mother, who told my mother, who gave me a bloody good hiding, again!

Another time I remembered being escorted by a policeman taking me home by the scruff of my neck, knocking on my front door my mother answered and got the fright of her life seeing me there with this 'Copper'. She went ballistic

"What the bloody hell you been up to this time you 'little horror' just get inside and I'll give you a thrashing!

"Hold on there Mrs, I found him running across the main road at the Princess Parade causing havoc with the traffic, he could have killed himself and anyone else that might have tried to avoid him.

You are responsible, what on earth is he doing out on his own anyway?

I didn, t know he was out of the house" said my Mother.

"Well you bloody well should have, I hold you responsible, do not hit your kid I'll be back to check on you" then he left.

I ran upstairs to my bedroom and put a chair behind the door handle. She immediately followed I could hear her clomping up the stairs shouting at the top of her voice "you bloody little sod, get me into trouble would you? I'll give you a thrashing", but she couldn't get in to my room, and then she would calm down threatening me with telling my Dad when he got home from work. But she never did and I never got that thrashing

My First Trike at Age Four and Monty

9 Red

Parents in the early fifties were so trusting compared with the society that we now lived in, especially with the hardships of the War which was only five years gone. There was a community spirit that looked out for everyone in our street. With *Mrs Ridgeyard* living across the road next to *Mrs Castings, the Murphys* on the corner with Jimmy my best mate (yes that jimmy) exactly one year younger than me and an Irish lad.

We had a lot of the Irish folks living on our estate; I guess they all came over to work in Fords (the motor foundry).

Never new the first names of our grown up neighbours, I guess it was the respect that we gave to the folks back then.................but as a kid I didn't know that at the time.

We also had the *'Roaches'* living next door, an Indian family, well that was the name my mother told me, *not Patel*!................ but then I doubt she could pronounce it anyway, the *Roaches* it was!

My mother would often complain about the smell of their cooking but to me it was gorgeous full of spices and aroma that just simply filtered through to our garden and beyond. They were a nice elderly couple and I got on well with them.

Our other immediate neighbours were *Geordies* they were great as well, had a nice quiet dog called *Monty*, who I befriended and he looked after me when I needed him. He's the one in the picture. Never knew their real name so I just called them the *Geordies*, I didn, t even know why?

There was the *'Malones', the 'Macholics' the 'Battersbys' the 'Holders'* and the *'Tadopes'* just to name but a few that I had run-ins with, during those spring and summer days of excitement as a kid. Further up the street, it was a long street...... lived the *'Steeles'* and the *'Stitts'*, Oh! and the compulsory old moaning woman on the corner next to the *Geordies* her name was' Mrs Corcoran' I think, plus a few more that I will probably will have to make up.

We always seemed to be fed well for some reason, probably something to do with my mother working at the local butchers in 'Broad Street'. She would always come home with 'sheep's hearts', liver, tripe and meat for pies that she would make and cook. Although occasionally she would lose her rag with my dad...... that's when he was here, sitting at the table having his dinner with all the family for a change. She would suddenly throw the bloody plate of food at him, always missing with the plate but contents landing all over him.....................oh no! Here we go again.
I would have an asthma attack and run into the front room and hide while the 'second world war' broke out again as it so frequently did in our house.

My dad smoked a pipe my sisters cigarettes, my mum and brother had more sense all of which conspired to make me asthmatic and very shy................words were difficult for me to express, so I am my mothers son and if I couldn't get my way...well the old ginger temper and tantrums would explode and of coarse it would be back to the bedroom locked in, a good hiding and left to die............that's how it seemed to me in those early years growing up in my house.

We kids always played out in the street after school and at weekends, making up our own games and annoying the neighbours, playing ball, smashing windows (unintentionally) running through the front gardens causing havoc............did I say respect earlier, well the intentions were good.

When the old street lamp lighter started his rounds (that's an old song, must be the Browns who recorded that, as I found out when I was older) then you knew it was time to go in..........but I always waited till my mother would run up the street calling me names shouting obscenities from the top of her lungs, grabbing me by my ear dragging me home with another hiding and straight to bed.
If I was unlucky I would have to wash first............. what sweet memories.

The Big people also started to talk about the King....................The King had just waved-off the then, Princess Elizabeth and Duke of Edinburgh, they boarded a jet plane for a state visit to Kenya, and a short holiday, at the famous Tree Tops Hotel. Shortly afterwards the King died and the funeral was held February 1952. The poor princess had to come back to England. I didn't understand all this but the funeral was shown on the BBC in glorious black and white.

Mother did give us some treats sometimes, with outings to the seaside. 'South end On Sea and Clacton'.
My brother and I had great times on the beach although I didn't like him much. I always thought he was 'Jewish' he just had that look with his long nose and big ears and a skinny frame and of coarse

every time I called him names I would get that customary clip around the ears. No wonder that I had to have an operation eventually, what with him and my mother slapping me so hard……………..

"So Tommy lift this up while I go and get a cat, and don't drop it"
 For someone so shy I just had a habit of giving orders to the other kids.
 In the roads adjacent to the kerbs were the storm drains, cast iron and very heavy.
 At seven years old I had a hatred of cats and this was my solution of eliminating them from my street. You have to remember that in 1952 not many folks had these domestic animals, I'm sure during the war when food was scarce ……………..well I leave that to the readers imagination.
I caught this tabby and cuddled it and when I got to 'Tommy' I would drop it down the drain, it didn't go without a fight, scratching and whining. "Ouch! Its scratched me Ginger" Tommy let go of the bloody drain but didn't pull his hand away quick enough, "bang" as it fell and he just caught his hand trapped beneath the drain, with the cat squealing in the water below and Tommy's hand trapped.
I managed to lift it slightly and he pulled his hand out.
It was badly bruised, fortunately not broken as I found out later from my mother who spoke to Tommy's mother. Once again I was given another hiding………………

In my child's mind I thought I was doing a good deed by putting cats down the drains I was also solving the rodent issue and everyone would be pleased with me……….

I soon learnt that was not the best idea that I ever had, even at seven years old.

I never gave it a thought where the cat went after the drain cover was replaced, but he wouldn't go hungry.....................

My school was 'Beam Bridge Primary' just up the road from where I lived about five minutes walk. All of us kids used to go on their own, none of this 'mums escort' like we have now. But then those times were different and folks didn't think anything of it.

I quite liked my school at the time with forty or so kids in each classroom, I don't think we were taught much, but then I was a slow learner. I got home from school one afternoon to find my mother had packed her bags and said "get your things together, I am taking you and your bother to Uncle Bert's and Auntie Kath's for a while. Why Mum? Because I said so, just do it"

My Uncle and Aunt lived in a big council house in Walthamstow, so we had to get the 87 bus to Barking and the 145 to Walthamstow on a Friday evening in the late summer of 1952. I didn't understand why we had to go, but my brother who was fourteen years old at the time did try to explain what had happened.

My parents had had another bust-up.

I found out when I was much older that she accused him of getting on his BMS motor-bike to Saffron Walden and having an affair with a 'Tart' as she called it. So much for his shift work.............must have been doing triple shifts!

We were welcomed 'I think' with open arms when we arrived. My mother must have planned this for some time as there were no phones in peoples' homes in those days.

This was also about the time I started to make regular visits to 'Great Ormond Street Children's Hospital' due to an ear infection, which turned out to be something more.

....
....

Beach Boy

Smiling Faces

Still Smiling!

16 Red

Episode 2 – The Walthamstow Years

Chapter 1

A Day out at the 'Gamages' Store East London

'Aunty Kath' prepared us a meal and I got to know my cousins.

'Roy,' who was about my age. 'Brian' who was 10, and 'Eileen' who was the oldest.

The house as I remembered had three floors and us boys' slept on the top floor, recipe for a disaster because we mucked about so much, fighting and doing what boys' did at that age.

Mum got me into their school and I was petrified. A new school at seven years old, strange neighbourhood, and bloody weird kids, down at 'Hazlemear' Avenue'.

My first day didn't begin very well. At playtime a bigger kid came over to me and said "Oy, you, ginger nut got any sweets?" and of coarse I said no, and with that he started to slap me about a bit, when suddenly I heard a voice say "leave him alone 'Nobby' otherwise I'll give you a thumping, that new kid is my cousin."

Brian came to my rescue.

I never forgot 'Nobby' and a week or so later I got my revenge.

I went to the local shop and bought some rubber strip with my sweets pocket money to make a sling for a catapult. Broke a piece off a tree in a Y shape and tied the rubber to make up the catapult, found a piece of plastic for the sling envelope and 'hey presto' I had a weapon.

I don't remember any kids at the time having these I was probably one of the first, due to my inventive and warped mind. Where other kids used hard rice or something whatever they could get hold of as a missile I used steel staples. I don't think it was ever my intention to hurt anybody with this weapon but I was a revengeful awful kid from a broken home ………………………no excuse really but that was the way it was.

Anyway one day after school I saw 'Nobby' walking down the road towards me and I just happened to have my catapult tucked into my back pocket of my dirty shorts and without hesitation fired off around of staples; he went down crying and then ran home to his mum.

Once again I found out later that he was hit in the forehead with one of the staples, but he was alright a bit of a head-ach, so even with the help of my cousin 'Nobby' he didn't bother me again.

Television was just coming into people's homes, to those that could afford it and we were lucky. My Uncle had just purchased one but the programmes were few. I remember the children's hour from five to six.

My favourite programmes were Roy Rogers, the Lone Ranger, Hopalong Cassidy singing cowboys and more. 'Watch with Mother' which included Muffin the Mule, Bill and Ben etc.

With the coming of the TV my imagination just use to grow as it probably did with most kids

Christmas of 1952 was strange as I didn't see my father but my mum compensated by telling 'Father Christmas' that I would like a cowboy outfit and some glove puppets for Christmas.

I was not disappointed I had a great time with my cousins we played the usual cowboy and Indians during that winter and I used to put on a puppet show with my glove puppets. I would make a 'Punch and Judy' set out of some cardboard get myself inside it and made shows up to entertain my mates. That was great fun and I was a happy little soldier………………until my mum said "we are going to hospital to have a look at that ear of yours", I didn't know it was 'crocked'

We got through the winter of 1952-53, spring arrived and it was time to play outside again……………at last.
The big interest this year was the Coronation of Queen Elizabeth II. All the parents were gearing themselves up for a massive street party.
June 2nd was the day and we kids would be dressed up in wonderful outfits made out of crepe paper. I was a 'Yeoman of the guards,' my brother said he was too old, so mum left him alone. We had loads of silly games and party hats. Street entertainers and a wonderful day was held by all…………………..I won second prize for my costume with a toy soldier as my prize.

The Coronation Photograph shows my brother Don in the front row second from the left with me the 'terrible terror' sitting to the right of him. My mother was somewhere at the back.
My sisters didn't come to the party, they were teenagers at the time I don't remember seeing them again for at least a year……………to my mind it sure seemed that long.

I always remember the happiness people felt with a new young Queen as our new head of state. Obviously with the dark days of the Second World War only eight years now passed, this was a new beginning for everyone with hope of a new future ahead, even though there were still many bridges to cross.

The coronation increased the sale of televisions, just like today when there is a main event like a football world cup, so some-things never change.

Cousin Roy and Myself in our Outfits

Me and my Brother (The early years)

Coronation Street Party – June 1953

23 Red

Knobbly Knee Contest

Ma and Pa

24 Red

Isle of Wight

"Roy! I think this is far enough, I'm getting tired now, and all those Trolley Busses don't miss us by much, that last one nearly knocked me over.

Yeh, I know but I don't know where we are.

Well!" I said "its getting dark and I want to go back home now, mum will give me a hiding if we don't turn around.

Look! There's a policeman ask him where our house is? He won't know" said Roy. "I'll ask him then, if your so scared, I'm not scared" he said, then we started fighting"....................our bikes fell into the road.

"Ok! You two! What are you doing out on your own on this busy road? The policeman asked. "We're! Lost Sir" I said. I was always respectful to the police.

So the nice policeman asked us where we lived and we gave him our address.

The next we knew a Black Maria turned up. Don't know why it was called that. But it was a black police van and they put our bikes in the back while we sat in the front all very excited now, because he wasn't going to take us to prison for being naughty, he was taking us home.

We arrived home about seven a clock and Uncle Bert was there to greet us, my mum was shopping, got away with that one. Uncle Bert was ok about it but he did give us both a ticking off and that was the end of it.

I got a second hand bike for my birthday I think my dad bought it for me, mum never said but my brother told me this............so it must have been true !

Saturday mornings were great, my cousins and I used to go along to the local street market just up the road from where we lived and go to the local 'Flea-Pit' a common name for the ABC cinema.

Pay our sixpence for the admission price and be in fantasy land for two hours.

On the way out we used to run 'amok'. Running down the road 'nicking' as much as we could hold in our hands from the 'street raders' stalls. Sweets, fruit and anything else that might be of some use for trading with other kids'. Always a profitable Saturday, until one of us would get caught, get a clip around the ear and sent on or way again. But it never stopped us. We were soon back for more the following week.

Chapter 2

Hospital Tales

My Mother decided to take me to the local doctors towards the autumn of 53' I was starting to have trouble with my right ear. The doctor recommended me to the 'Great Ormond Street Children's Hospital' in London to see a specialist. Something about an infection, that could lead to complications.

We got the 'Trolley bus' to the hospital. I just loved those buses. They were so smooth with their overhead rods attached to the power lines above. Quiet running engines and very comfortable.

In Dagenham we didn't have those buses they were special to the 'big smoke' (London). I always wanted to go upstairs but my mother said "NO" too smoky, would make my asthma worst". She couldn't control the smokers at home though! Had to put up with that............and deteriorating health.

So we saw the specialist and his conclusions were "he has a growth on the bone in his inner year, which is obviously causing him pain, in other words a 'Mastoid'. He will need to come in for an operation. However I must point out to you Mrs Ryder that this operation is in its pioneering stage at the moment. We will have to open up his right ear, almost removing it to get inside to the bone and remove the area of bone that is infected. It could be so close to the nerve tissue and may cause permanent facial disfiguration"

'Crash Bang'.......................

That was my mother fainting and falling to the floor.

started crying, not because of what I heard, because I didn't understand it anyway. But because my mother had suddenly died………………….that's what I thought, until the smelling sorts arrived with a nurse and sat her back up again.

On the way out we walked over to 'Gamages' and she bought me an ice-cream and a toy, so I was happy for a while.

 was admitted to the hospital around about January of 54' eight and a half years old.

We moved back to Dagenham, I went back to my old school and Mum and Dad tried to play at happy families. My Sister 'Iris' had to grovel to our mother if she wanted to come back and stay with us again. Mother told her to ask dad if it was alright to move back in. He of course said it was ok, but my mother held a grudge against her because she didn't come to Walthamstow with us.
Maggie' my other sister was ok no problems, she was allowed back.
Both my sisters were teenagers at the time and did have jobs, so the extra income into the household was welcomed. Also my bother at fifteen started an apprenticeship at 'Fords' as an electrician.

I was at my old school until January then it was off to the hospital. The 'Green line' bus took us all the way.
I was admitted in; when they told my mother the operation would probably be in a few days, and to come back then. I didn, t stop crying…………………….

'Drink it all down Peter" said the nurse,

29 Red

"But its orrible, I don't like it,

It's good for you, she said.

No it isn't, if it was, I would like it" but I drank it all down anyway. Pre-op medicine and they starved me for hours and hours…………………..

I was wheeled into the operation theatre and a masked was put over my mouth………..that was it; I was out for the count. From that moment on I never wanted to experience that feeling again.

When eventually I woke up, I was not alone. My Mother was sitting in the corner of the room. She had been here all night and had slept in the 'parents room' the hospital arrange this for the parents of children that have operations.

She didn't scream, so I guess my face wasn't disfigured.

However when I mention this in my adult life all my mates take the 'Pee' and say "you sure about that?"

So I spend many weeks in hospital, with check-ups and baths and further check-ups. As you can imagine boredom takes its toll on an eight year old kid.

I see a lot of kids in my ward with all kinds of ailments. I remember walking into the ward at the end of the corridor, with that smell of medicine and disinfectant and blood. There was this kid in one of the beds with blood just pouring out of his mouth a doctor I presumed was holding a gigantic pair of faucets, pushing it down the poor kid's throat and pulling lumps of 'something' out of his mouth……………I woke up after fainting, with a nurse telling me I shouldn't have been here and that this kid had tonsil problems, didn't mean anything to me............. but a lasting memory remained.

My room was very bright with lots of toys and books to read, I started to feel at ease. There was a door that opened out to the balcony and when the sun was shining, my favourite nurse would take me out here for some fresh-air. But this one day she got distracted, so I went back in and locked the door behind her and ran off. I found another kid to play with and totally forgot she was out there.

At tea-time there was a hell of a commotion. The ward sister and my favourite nurse caught up with me. Fortunately they couldn't clip me around the ear, but what a verbal bashing they gave me. My favourite nurse had been locked out for nearly six hours, it was February and cold and she was not very amused.

was given the all clear after about two months and left the hospital, but had to come back every three months or so for further check-ups................I didn't go back to school again until after the summer break.

Chapter 3

The summer of 1954

The summer of '54' was once again a good summer.

You know you always remember that the days were warm and the skies were blue and fun was had by all, could be a cue for a song!

"Tommy how long are we gonna keep throwing these stones at ginger? Screamed James, "until he gives in and shouts for 'Fein lights', then it's our turn"

There were still these 'Anderson war shelters' in our gardens and most of the parents were either using them as coal bunkers or dismantling them for other uses. So we kids came along with this idea of rebuilding them badly with one of us inside and pelting him with stones. The noise was excruciating. The one who stayed in the longest was a real hero…………………………the one who squealed the most was banished from our little gang and sent off crying his eyes out, that's of coarse providing he hasn't been hit by a stone and sent to hospital in-stead.

We also used to take these sections of corrugated sheets over the park and use them as sledges for sitting on and sliding down the hills, racing and crashing in to each other.

A favourite pastime was to wade into the local river and retrieve some old prams that were thrown away. We would make go-carts out of them and race around the streets – great fun. When we were bored with this we used to go along the New Road (A13) to a local factory to scrounge some ball bearing wheels. These were for the start of a new craze in self made scooters. Made out of scrap timber added mechanical parts and 'hey-presto' a new toy was invented. Fortunately my dad always seemed to have a lot of timber in his shed. So with a saw and a hammer we were up and running.

We would find a hill and race down, making wonderful noises, crashing into each other and overshooting into the main road, narrowly missing the oncoming traffic. Then back again for another run. This would last until the inevitable 'Policeman' would arrive and stop all the fun.

Saturday mornings was the outing to the 'Princess Cinema' for the kids' club movies. Two hours of 'Flash Gordon and the Cavemen' the 'Range Rider' followed by 'Lassie' and 'Mighty Mouse' absolutely looked forward to these shows. The noise was deafening and not a spare seat in the house. But there were always gate crashers. The 'EXIT' double doors would be flung open just as we sat down and a group of kids would dash in, disappearing into the cinema.

Before I left for the cinema I would always sneak a look in to my mother's purse when she wasn't looking and see how much loose change she had. Without hesitation I would 'nick' a couple of shillings or half-a-crown. Treat myself to a box of 'Payne's Poppet's' chocs, before going into see the films and afterwards an ice-cream or pommygramite'. You get pips with a 'Pommy' so I could have a spitting fight with the other kids.

This was also the year that I joined the 'Cubs'. Mum and Dad bought me the uniform but my motives were not what they expected. I would go on the normal camping weekends and stay in those Hugh 'bell tents' with the other kids, but it wasn't for me. To regimental and strict, but I used to like going along to the local 'Co-op 'hall and have fun and games with my mates. 'Bob-a-Jobbing' was my favourite bit. I would always bring in the most money during the season and thought to myself - 'what a waste'. So I came up with an entrepreneurial idea. I would do the tasks and pocket the money for myself.

I would make up a card, nicely painted with all the columns inside for my customers to sign and date just like normal, wear my cub uniform, with the nice green jersey, hat and toggle scarf and I was set up for my mission.

'Ring, ring' I pressed the door bell on the front porch at number 32 Second avenue and a nice old lady came to the door.

"Hello young man" she croaked.

"Hello! and good morning to you, Missus. I was wondering if you had any jobs I could do, to help my 'Cub pack' cos we are trying to collect money to build a new hall for old people in the community etc, etc.

What a nice young man, yes! I do have some chores for you – come in .You could first lay this table out for me and set it for dinner for four people, my son and his wife together with my grand-daughter will be here tonight and then you could cut the grass."

It was part of our training to set out dining tables with the correct cutlery and so on – 'what a bore' but if I could get money from doing these kinds of chores for my good neighbours, then it was well worth it.

After about an hour I was finished. "Missus I have finished,

Well done young man," she was about to let me out without paying 'bloody cheek' so I had to ask her for some money "Missus this is 'Bob-a-Job week and you are suppose to pay me for these jobs,

Oh I forgot" she croaked again, "How much is it?" So I thought "well normally it's a shilling (a bob) but as I have done so much, make it hree bob" and she paid. I gave her my card to sign and then she said but this card is not like the real ones. I know, I filled the last one up and made this one myself,

What a clever lad you are" she croaked again " I will have to inform your troupe 'Arkala' on what a jolly good advance thinking boy you are – I said please don't missus" and then darted out of her house to ook for the next mug.

was kicked out of the Cubs when eventually Akala found out, but it didn't stop me from 'Bob-a-Jobbing'. I made quite a bit of 'dosh' out of his little scam to buy loads of sweets and comics

On the wet days of summer I would spend my time staying in and entering painting competitions that were always advertised in the Knockout and Beano' comics. I was relatively successful winning water colour paint sets and the pride of my trophies' 'A Davy Crocket Racoon hat'. The film 'Davy Crocket' had just arrived in the cinemas' here, and what a treat this was. Had to queue for two hours to get in and see it at the 'Heathway Odeon' on a hot Saturday afternoon. And hereafter I would became 'Davy Crocket' king of the wild frontier, rom Tennessee USA, born on a mountain top and killed a Bear when ne was only three. The song went something like that – and then Batman' and 'Superman 'came along in the DC comics which started another craze

We would often cycle to 'Ockendon' woods. Tommy, Jimmy, Freddie and me. Mom would always ask me to stay around the area. I suppose she felt we were safer here but she couldn't keep an eye on ne all the time and of coarse I didn't care anyway.

council house in Barking, and no benefits were handed out by the government of the day. That word hadn't even been invented then.

At weekends everyone would be here, Gran-Ma would lay on the tea with the help of her two daughters. All the brothers and sisters and their kids, then Gran-Ma would roll out the piano and we would have a party singing all the songs of the war, 'pack-up your troubles in your old kit bag and smile-smile-smile' followed by 'knees-up mother brown' and many more. Crikey she was good on the old 'ivories' (piano) and I just loved it and never wanted to go home. We would even do the 'conga' out in the street with the neighbours joining in. All this without any alcohol, oh what fun! When it all quietened down the playing cards would come out, but they wouldn't let me join in. Mum took me home on the bus and that was the end for this day, but these were quite frequent events and I would always look forward to the next time.

I had a toothache. Mum said I'll take you to see the Dentist. I thought it was just like going to see the doctors. No problem there then. But oh! How wrong was I?

Sitting in the waiting room I could smell the hospital smell all over again. Puke, disinfectant and all the memories of my hospital days were coming back to haunt me.

We entered the dentist's room and I sat down in the chair.........He looked into my mouth, had a prod and then told my mother that I had an abscess and that he would need to take out the offending tooth which was at the back of my jaw on the lower set. I thought 'oh Jesus' not again.

I started to faint, but he put something under my nose and then I came around again. "OK Peter, be a brave little soldier, I will put this mask over your nose and mouth and you won't feel a thing, soon be over"

He Gassed me!!!.

woke up and there was blood everywhere. Swabs were going into my mouth like sweets off a trolley. He said to my Mum take him home and just keep changing the dressings. It would not stop bleeding and what with me keep passing out; Mum had a full time job dealing with t.

From that day on the fear of ever going to a Dentist just scared the sh** out of me.

Tommy and I started hunting in the hedges of the gardens down our road. We were looking for these huge green caterpillars with horns at the end of their bodies. Hadn't a clue what they were called but in the summer months it was fun collecting them. I used to go out with a jar and put one of these caterpillars in. I didn't kill it I wasn't that cruel to Mother Nature, just cats! I would add a twig, a large privet leaf and put the lid back on with air holes, and then as autumn approached magic happened. The caterpillar turned into a cocoon and eventually a giant moth. Wow! That really impressed me. Obviously, I would remove the lid and let him fly away. But that little section of nature never failed to impress me.

Me – 9 Years Old (Big Ears)

**Uncle Ben, Ma, Uncle Wal, Aunt Doris, Uncle Bill, Uncle Bert
and Uncle Len – approx. 1964**

"Mrs Ryder please come in and sit down ". Anyway the outcome was I had to see a school Psychiatrist, to monitor my behaviour and to weekly do mental test to see if I was barmy or something. This went on for about six weeks, until finally he reported to the headmaster and my mum.

"There is nothing wrong with the lad" he stated, "just high spirited and that's due to his lack of expression with words, lets his temper get the better of him", and so on and so on…………..

So I was alright, as if I cared. I carried on as normal, but my mum although very pleased, still had mixed emotions about the outcome

In fact she decided it was now time that I should get a religious education. She enrolled me into the local Church for Sunday school. I had to wear my best togs and attend the church in old Dagenham High Street. First time she would take me and when she got bored with that would make me go on my own, what a mistake! Naturally it wasn't 'my cup of tea' as the saying goes………I would obviously bunk off, and spend my Sunday school money on treats, instead of giving it to the Vicar, I would buy some comics and go to the local swings, hang around for a couple of hours before going back home. Unfortunately my mother found out, the Vicar came round to our house and complained to Mum. I didn't have to go again.

However she got her revenge from that day on I was grounded on Sundays, never to step outside again to play with my mates. I just stared out of the front window feeling sorry for myself all the time. My mates would knock on the front door and she would just turn them away.

t was in that summer that I had a new idea. I would go out and play on Saturday and take to drinking milk, but of course I wasn't going to pay for it! so I would help myself to the neighbours milk, steal it from outside their front door. It used to be delivered in pint bottles by the milkman on his horse and carriage, I would creep into the neighbours gardens and 'half inch (pinch) it. But the best trick was to take the top off, have a few sips, then put the bottle back, my warped sense of humour thought this was really cool. I use to imagine the look on the neighbours faces when they picked up their milk. This was one trick I never got caught at, Whoopee.

Back at school I started to get interested in the girls...........I was only 9 or 10 and they would always be playing their stupid games in the playground. I don't know why but for some reason I was just interested, maybe the challenge of them liking me, because nobody else did. Attention seeking I suppose. Anyway I knew my mother had a jewellery box in her bedroom full of sparkling brooches and the like and I just thought they would be the kind of ornament that girls might like. Had no idea of what they might cost, but I was sure my mother would not miss one or two, she literally had hundreds, seemed like that to me anyway! So I would choose the prettiest and give it to the girl of my choice- 'Wow' I soon became popular, so popular in fact every week I would have to give another broach away, until finally my mother's jewellery box was only half full................oh dear, looks like I am in trouble again. So I stopped. Strangest thing but mother never said anything about her amazing disappearing brooches. So that was another naughty I got away with. It taught me that if you take things gradually over time, then you can get away with it, but of course I was never proud of this – 'I was only a kid.'

When November the 5th arrived I would buy some fireworks, usually *bangers and firecrackers* and scare the daylights out of the other kids by throwing the lighted fireworks at them. But the worst thing I did was really bad and I sometimes wonder how nothing bad resulted from my actions. In our street some houses had a driveway that lead to an alley. The front doors of these houses were faced directly opposite each other, with a space of about 10 metres apart. So I would get a piece of string tie the front door knockers together, that way they could not open their front doors. Then with that action completed I would light the firecrackers and put one each through the letter box, knock on their doors and run away to hide to see what would happen. This would be early evening and therefore dark. The front rooms of the houses would light up with the firework display, as the owners rushed to their front doors to open them, and of course they couldn't. They would eventually put out the firecracker and then race to their back door to get out. Oh! I did have a laugh and a giggle. But what a stupid thing to do…………..

Christmas was on its way again and my Dad and sister Maggi would always pay for me to go to their works Christmas children parties. Fords foundry and Dagenham Cables were the venues. It would always be in the works canteens and they were huge. Must have been hundreds of kids, plenty of grub and we would all get to see Santa with a present given to all the kids, not forgetting the compulsory apple and orange to take home, a rarity for those days.

always looked forward to the boys annuals at Christmas. Once again seemed to get what I wanted. *Superman, Batman, the Beano* and as many marvel comics that could fill my Christmas sack

Winters were horrible No TV for kids accept between the hours of 5.0 m and 6, I was allowed to stay up to 8/9 o'clock. TV was hardly ever on once the novelty wore off, but weekends' was the time we would watch it the most. I use to shut myself into the front room and play games with my toy soldiers and cowboys.

A new Sci-fi TV programme was about to start, called *'Quatermass and the Pit'* and I was allowed to watch it. The programme started about 8.0 pm. It was about a returning Spaceman in a rocket, but his two other Astronauts' were turned to dust. He started to turn into a cactus and weird things were going on at the local underground station. Frightened the life out of me…………..I ran upstairs and started to have nightmares. Ma wouldn't let me watch that programme again.

used to love reading my comics but the only problem was that once read, that was it. Leave them for a few weeks and then read them again. However I came up with a real ingenious plan. On Saturday afternoons I would trot down to Broad Street to the local newspaper and sweetshop and with my saved pocket money or the shilling that I found in my Mums' purse I would browse over the comics at the back of the shop, pick one up and put two others in the middle. Walk over to the cashier and pay for the one comic. It worked every time, that's what you really call buy one get the other two for free.

Ma and Pa's Wedding Photo 5th August 1934

(Granma and Ma's sister at the back)

The Baylis Clan

(About 1941)

Top Row: Bill, Bert and wife Kath, Len, Ben and wife Daisy, Pa
(holding my brother Don)

Second Row: Ma, Albert, Granma, Granddad, Jack (husband of) Doris

Bottom Row: Iris and third from left Maggi

Chapter 5

1955

'Tommy, stand next to me here, then when Jimmy comes around the corner of the building you run the other way and I'll jump, he will never catch us.' We kids were playing on a building site, one floor up close to the A13 where some new houses were being built. This area was bombed during the war, with old 'Hitler's Doodle Bugs raining down to try and devastate the Fords works where many of the military hardware was manufactured. We would often come here and play probably very dangerous but we had great fun running over the scaffold, up and down the ladders playing 'touch'. I would often jump from the first floor level into the sand mound at the ground level trying to imitate 'Batman' with my sidekick 'Robin' close behind me. Only trouble with that was he would always jump to early and therefore land on top of me – but who cared, just a few bumps and bruises with nothing broken, well!, most of the time anyway.

It would always seem that in the six weeks summer holidays it rained. At home, or when I was on holiday with my parents at Great Yarmouth. This year we stayed at a B and B on the seafront somewhere, but of course after 10.0 am they would throw us out, so we had to do something. Go to the pier and spend money in the penny arcades. I started to upgrade my comic reading at about this time and buy comic classics. These were like books for children, a comic but stories of Robinson Crusoe, Wuthering Heights, Robin Hood etc. they certainly kept me engrossed until it stopped raining

There was never any other children, for me to play with, so these summer breaks with my parents were totally boring, couldn't get up to any mischief. I used to look forward to getting back home and go out to play with the other kids

Ma – Unusually posing on the Promenade Great Yarmouth

School Photo

Hop Picking Holiday 1953

Ma and Pa at the back, Myself and Don at the front

52 Red

Granddad Baylis died in November this year. He left some money to my Grandma and the dear old lady divided it all up to leave equal shares to all her grandchildren. In later years I discovered the amount was £1168 (todays figure with inflation averaging about 3%, £73000) which was quite a huge amount at that time. My mother told me that a post office account had been set up for me and that she had donated £150 into my account. When I found this out I obviously wanted to spend it now, but of course that was never going to happen. In later years it was to become very helpful.

Chapter 6

1956

This was my last year at Beam-bridge school and I was really upset that I would be leaving and going to the big school 'Marley' after the holidays. All the kids said that the older boys would beat us up before and after school, so obviously this scared us a great deal, and we all get upset again.................

To celebrate this last term the school organised a trip to Guernsey an island in the channel and asked the parents to pay for it. I wasn't sure if I wanted to go or not, but Ma and Pa as always new better and thought it would be educational for me, so I was definitely going.

We departed early June from Southend airport. Crikey! This was daunting, never seen an aeroplane before and now I was going to fly in one. I suppose I was excited, but apprehensive as well. This was definitely a whole new ballgame and we kids were about as noisy as you would expect.

The officials dropped a ladder down from the fusillade and we all clambered up to get on board. We all sat 2 by 2 and got strapped in for the 45 minute journey for the 'up in the sky' experience.

I don't remember there been a proper runway. This thing just revved up and made a lot of noise as it was about to take off. I heard one of the teachers saying that this aeroplane was a twin engine prop jet called a 'Dakota' and was used a lot at the end of the war to transfer all the troops back from Germany.

It was a lovely June morning and we took off over towards the sea and could see the Southend pier below us – Wow! What a sight. It idn't take long and we were soon about to land in Guernsey. The oise was deafening and as we approached the runway to land, omething was not quite right. The teachers were shouting at us all to e quiet, but we took no notice, when suddenly the wheels hit the round, the tail part of the plane was whisking from side to side, all us ids were now screaming and hanging on to each other for dear life, he fusillade was jumping up and down and the brakes of the plane vere droning very excitably when suddenly we stopped – everyone vent quiet, the captain came out (there was no intercom) and said verything is fine , so please remain seated while we open the door nd then you can all leave the plane and walk back to the airport erminal, children with your teachers. 'Unfortunately' the Captain said have overshot the runway and landed in a potato field, and that was vhy it was so bumpy when we hit the ground, but don't worry verything is fine'.

Ve exited the plane on an emergency chute, one by one hitting the round until finally all walking back to the Terminal.

'ut me off from flying for quite some time after that – the girls were uking up everywhere, but the boys - well! They all behaved as boys vould behave, poking fun at the girls and having a jolly good laugh.

After that excitement we were all put on buses and journeyed to our odgings to Roquaine Bay camp.

Vhat a place – more like a German prisoner of war barracks with long uts, the boys in one, and the girls in the other. It wasn't just our chool. It included schools from other regions, seemed like hundreds. Twenty beds along both sides, what a noise, what a fiasco. We must ave been sent here for punishment

About the only thing I can remember about that trip, is when we all had an outing to the German underground military hospital, which had quite an effect on me at the time

All you can see above ground is the entrances and the square holes which are the escape shafts.

Construction started in the winter of 1940 - the first winter of the Occupation.

The tunnels were dug out by hundreds of slave workers from France, Spain, Morocco, Algeria, Belgium, Holland, Poland, Russia and Guernsey.

The Guernsey men refused to work after a rock fall killed six Frenchmen and were transferred elsewhere.

The slave labourers were given a simple choice - work or starve. Any who were too weak to work were sent to a detention camp in Alderney.

To dig the tunnels the workers had to use not only explosives and pneumatic drills but picks, shovels, sledge hammers and bare hands.

The German Military Underground Hospital and Ammunition Store took three and a half years of work before it was ready.

One grave digger had to bury seventeen workers killed in an explosion. They joined 37 men and women in a cemetery adjoining a workers' camp at Les Vauxbelets.

Iron escape ladder.

56 Red

Some of the granite excavated was used in the concrete. Amongst the 15,000 tons of concrete was British cement captured at Dunkirk.

The rest of the stone was transported along the light railway tracks in the tunnels and dumped across the road.

The granite was thrown into the valley and the ground level was raised as a result.

Work stopped when the D-Day battle began.

The hospital was built in two sections

The channels in the floors were not properly finished and are to deal with the damp which must have been a problem from the start.

Entrances were camouflaged to blend in with the surrounding countryside.

The 2nd larger section was also built as wards with an extra corridor in the middle which was blocked, increasing the storage area.

There were three tunnel entrances and five ventilation shafts with iron ladders or concrete steps so they could be used as emergency exits.

They range in depth from 45 feet to 75 feet. The 75 foot shaft has a reservoir dug into one side which could hold thousands of gallons of water.

The water was pumped into the reservoir from the nearby well and gave the compound an independent water source.

During the construction many German wagons were used on Guernsey roads drawn by French and Belgian horses.

After the liberation the British government sold off the wagons and horses.

Arthur this year, so was pleased to see him here. My other mates were all Catholics and so they all went to a Catholic School, a bus ride away. This was the start of losing those mates and trying to find new ones, and I was not very good at that.

All the new starters were told to stay behind and we were separated into three categories. Class A, B and C. Poor Arthur went into class C, while Harry and I were class A. I thought why put me there, I'm bloody useless and I know I will struggle

We were all marched down the corridor to class 1A, 44 of us to the science lab. Mr Lions our teacher, we were all told was the best.

It was all rather strange to me, because we would only spend the first hour with him, for the monitor form to be marked, the bell would ring and in accordance with our school timetable system march off to another class and teacher for other subjects.
September 1956 a whole new world and now my education really does begin

Chapter 7

The Summer of 1957

I used to spend a lot of time kicking a ball around in our small garden, until eventually I happened to break a window. My mother as usual went berserk clipping me around the head, complaining how much this was going to cost. I gave her a kick in her varicose veins and started to run indoors and upstairs where once again I locked myself in to my brother's bedroom. My Sisters had moved out by then and were staying locally on the estate somewhere, so we now had our own bedrooms. Mother came rushing up the stairs, but couldn't get in. She was mad and I just kept quiet until she had decided to go back down again. I had a 'mosey' around in my brother's wardrobe and found an old cigar box. Lifted the lid up and Wow! Lots of 'Godivers' (fivers) were in there. Now to a 'tea-leaf' like me that was tempting providence. I thought he wouldn't miss one if I took it, call it borrowing. To me it was like a small fortune, and I guess it was. It would be like fifty pounds or more today with inflation. So I grabbed one, went over to the window and opened it, then climbed down the drainpipe at the front of the house so mother wouldn't see me and ran. I met Jimmy and Tommy and said 'fancy a trip to the seaside It's on me we will have a great day' they obviously jumped at it – so we were off on an adventure with no parents to have a go at us.

We three walked to Dagenham Dock railway station, about 15 minutes away and I purchased the tickets to South End, bought some sweets and crisps and then boarded the next train, we were off.

Journey was about 45 minutes and we were very noisy the whole journey but fortunately had the carriage to ourselves.

First port of call was the 'Kursal'. Had a ride on the Big Dipper, ghost train and a few other rides. But they did cost a lot of money so we decided to go to 'Peter Pans' playground, which was along the promenade about 10 minutes' walk away. Bought some ice creams and we were so happy, what great fun, like playing truant from school I guess, not that I ever did, but Tommy had, so I guess it was like that

'Jimmy I'll race you and Tommy to the crazy house with the mirrors' my favourite. When Ma brought me here we would always go to this venue. It made fat people thin and thin people fat, never stopped laughing. I was well out in front when suddenly I heard a voice say 'Peter what are you doing here' I turned around and to my complete amazement sore Uncle Bert and Aunty Kath.................'Where is your Mum'? He shouted 'you're not here on your own, are you? no of course not. I've just ran ahead she is somewhere behind me, but I can't stop, in a hurry! Bye.'

'Sh*.t! I thought what a mess, fancy seeing them here, what if they tell Ma.......but then again it could be months before they see my Ma again and by then they would all forget, I hope.'

I was really worried this time. Mum would ask me a lot of questions about where did I get the money? Who was I with? And she probably thinks I am still imprisoned in my brother's bedroom...............oh crikey, I don't know how I will get out of this one.

Met up with Tommy and Jimmy and told them about it, but of course they couldn't care less. They didn't steal the money from my brother!!

soon got over it and we all started to enjoy ourselves again, but on the return to the railway station we all kept a wide berth of the promenade – just in case.

Finally got home early evening, and tried to sneak in. She was there. 'Where the bloody hell have you been all day' she screamed. Her face was the colour of a fire engine, with the bell ringing at full volume. 'No-where I said, just out playing, to get away from you, you Old Cow'! What did you say?' I ran and dodged her again and stormed up the stairs to my bedroom and this time I was not coming out until the morning, Phew!

Another great day out was to go to the Rainham sand pits, especially on a hot summers day. A few of us would trek through the Millhouse grounds along the new road. It was about 30 minutes' walk. Once here we would find a secluded spot and take our clothes off for a bit of skinny dipping, as it was affectionately called. This was really fun, even though the signs read 'Keep Out' deep water. I was not a really good swimmer, but doggy paddled and hoped for the best. How dangerous was that? We were all mad to do this. The water was really deep but fortunately nobody ever got in to trouble.

What a special year this was going to be. My Sister Iris was going to get married to a guy in the Army. She brought him home a few times to meet the parents, a very gregarious guy and I warmed to him straight away. It could have been because of the nice presents he would always bring me I suppose.

The wedding was set for some time in August and I think they pencilled me in to be a page-boy. I don't know where my parents found the money to pay for the wedding, but at least we didn't have to go on another boring holiday

Loads of activity, people going and coming, I had never seen our house like this before. Ma and Iris making all the arrangements, Church, dress and reception to organise until finally the big day had arrived. Sis looked amazing, like a Hollywood movie star, I just couldn't believe how beautiful she looked. I can only remember things in black and white. We didn't have colour in those days so I guess that was the way it was, it was natural to think like that, and I suppose most people did. I had my 'Whistle and Flute' (suit) on, and everyone wanted to pinch by baby face cheek, crikey that was embarrassing, I just wish they would leave me alone and concentrate on my sister.

The cars arrived, so we all got in them while my Sis and Pa followed up in the rear car. This was all really exciting. I had never been to a Wedding before let alone my own Sister's, and travelling in these nice black cars as well.

We arrived at the Church in Old Dagenham. Everyone was there, it was packed to the rafters and after a short wait the music of 'here comes the bride' filled the church and beyond, just wonderful, I was knocked out by the whole spectacle of all this. Then my Sis walked down the aisle with Pa and she finally stood next to her future husband 'Eddie'
It was just wonderful and very emotional as well. Don't remember the hymns but I did sing along with great enthusiasm.

After the ceremony we all congregated outside 'as you do' to take the family photos. Then all back to Blakes Avenue Barking to the Scouts hall for the 'bash'.

A good knees up was had by all, until my mother came over and said Uncle Bert had told her about me at the Southend trip, 'I'll sort you out later 'she said to me. Oh dear a brilliant day now tarnished with a threat from my mother

66 Red

August 1957- The Wedding

ow. Neighbour, Eddie's brother, Dorothy, Me, Pamela, Ed's mum, Eddie and Sis,

Pa, Maggi (my sister) Grandma, neighbours

d row. Maurice, Donald (my brother) and the rest were friends and neighbours

What a luvly Picture!

'OK you little bugger, explain yourself. What were you doing at Southend and   did this have anything to do with your Brother's missing fiver? Shouted my Mother, 'and don't lie'.

I don't know anything about my Brothers missing fiver. I had a bit of pocket money, so did Jimmy and Tommy, and between us we had a day out at the seaside. That was all. Uncle Bert was there and he saw me. I didn't do anything wrong'

'I don't believe you, but you better be on your best behaviour for quite a long time now, or your Father will hear about this one, and he 'will' give you a good hiding, OK!' I said, and then went out to play. As if I was worried about Pa, it's my Mother that worries me, she's bonkers!

Chapter 8
The Winter of 1957-58

I didn't get beaten up at school, so that was a relief. Managed to avoid all the bigger boys and found some lads to play with and we got along just fine

The long cold nights in winter were always horrible. Although we kids would often go to the Night Watchman's hut and keep warm around the fire. There would often be road works around our streets and at night a man had to look after the area. He would sit all night long in a steel fabricated hut with a fire burning in a cage. He was always an old cheerful boy, and he would like the company of us kids. We would roast potatoes on his fire and have a good old sing-song. It was really fun, so this was a regular past-time in the evenings.

Swapping comics with other kids, model making from my Air fix kit, usually ships and planes and that was it really. No TV to watch, not for children anyway.

There was this black dog that I sometimes used to see in the streets, and I kind of took a shine too. I would save some of my dinner and take it to him and we would become great pals. He was my protector I used to feel really invincible when we were together. As soon as I came out of my house I would walk up the road to where he lived , and if he wasn't outside I would call him, unfortunately I didn't know his name, so I just whistled and named him Blackie.

Out he would bound, almost knocking me over, licking me almost to death. We had great adventures over the parks, down the rivers. He was always with me when I was out. There were times when other nasty kids thought they could have a go at me; it didn't last for long, 'Blackie, attack! Bite them boy' and he would go for them and bite their legs. Nasty kids soon ran away and I suddenly discovered what power this was with my friend beside me.

Fireworks night was always great, with many Bonfires in the back-gardens of our neighbourhood. On one particular occasion Blackie was provoked by a kid called Percy Knight. Blackie bit him and unfortunately his mother saw this happen. Me and Blackie ran away and I thought that would be the end of it, but a few weeks later when I walked up the road to get him, I whistled and a man came out of his house and said my dog won't be coming out to play anymore with you son. 'Why'? I said,

'Because, he bit one person to many, and we had to send him away',

What do you mean, when will he be back?'

'Son, he has gone to heaven, he won't be back'

'Oh jeez, I couldn't stop crying…………….but I suppose it was my fault. I taught Blackie some good tricks but also some bad tricks and now he has gone forever

Blackie

71 Red

Christmas was around the corner again and George Formby was all the rage now, a funny man who could sing and play a Banjo. So obviously, I had this on my Xmas shopping list. And sure enough I was not disappointed. Ma and Pa always managed to buy me what I wanted with the help of my Sisters

The 6th February 1958 a date etched in my memory forever. I had just started to take interest in football. My brother would often go to see West Ham play, and he would take me with him sometimes. But on this date a disaster struck the Manchester United team and I remember reading the Sunday 'News of the World'. I just couldn't put the paper down. I was devastated with this news and totally horrified that something like this could happen. Unbelievable, shell shocked and a lasting image that has remained with me to this day. From that day onwards I became a Manchester United supporter. There was never going to be another team as far as I was concerned. Nearly 'West Ham United' due to the close proximity of the ground, but from that day onwards everything changed.

The **Munich air disaster** occurred on 6 February 1958, when British European Airways Flight 609 crashed on its third attempt to take off from a slush-covered runway at Munich-Riem Airport in Munich, West Germany. On board the plane was the Manchester United football team, nicknamed the "Busby Babes", along with a number of supporters and journalists. Twenty of the 44 people on board the aircraft died in the crash. The injured, some of whom had been knocked unconscious, were taken to the <u>Rechts der Isar Hospital</u> in Munich where three more died, resulting in a total of 23 fatalities with 21 survivors.

The team was returning from a <u>European Cup</u> match in <u>Belgrade</u>, <u>Yugoslavia</u> (now <u>Serbia</u>), against <u>Red Star Belgrade</u>, but had to make a stop in Munich for refuelling, as a non-stop trip from Belgrade to Manchester was out of the "Elizabethan" class <u>Airspeed Ambassador</u> aircraft's range. After refueling, the pilots, Captains James Thain and Kenneth Rayment, attempted to take off twice, but had to abandon both attempts due to boost surging in the port engine. Fearing that they would get too far behind schedule, Captain Thain rejected an overnight stay in Munich in favour of a third take-off attempt. By the time of the third attempt, it had begun to snow, causing a layer of slush to build up at the end of the runway. When the aircraft hit the slush, it lost velocity, making take-off impossible. It ploughed through a fence past the end of the runway, before the port wing hit a nearby house and was torn off. Fearing that the aircraft might explode, Captain Thain set about getting the surviving passengers as far away as possible. Despite this threat, Manchester United <u>goalkeeper</u> <u>Harry Gregg</u> remained behind to pull survivors from the wreckage.

An investigation by the West German airport authorities originally blamed Captain Thain for the crash, claiming that he had failed to de-ice the wings of the aircraft, despite statements to the contrary from eyewitnesses. It was later established that the crash had, in fact, been caused by the build-up of slush on the runway, which had resulted in the aircraft being unable to achieve take-off velocity;

Thain's name was eventually cleared in 1968, ten years after the incident.

At the time of the disaster, Manchester United were trying to become only the third club to win three successive English league titles; they were six points behind League leaders Wolverhampton Wanderers with 14 games to go. They were also holders of the Charity Shield and had just advanced into their second successive European Cup semi-final. The team, were also on an 11-match unbeaten run, and had booked their place in the Fifth Round of the FA Cup two weeks previously.

Chapter 9

A typical school day could be hilarious or it could be painful. On 'PE' days it was 'painful'. In midwinter our teacher would take the class down to the local outdoor swimming pool *'Leys'*. We would all have to change in unheated rooms and then rush out to the pool and jump in and learn to swim. I used to think this was crazy. Why didn't we all suffer from pneumonia? It was torture; all the teachers should have been arrested. Talk about health and safety, nobody had heard about it then. The problem for me of course was that I would get asthma attacks and back then nobody cared a 'Hoot. Let the children suffer was their motto. After one hour of this it was then time to get our clothes on and buy a nice cup of Bovril then head back to our warm classrooms.

A regular visit to see the travelling school nurse was always a nuisance, although it did get us out of the classroom for a few hours. The nurse would have to prod our scalps and have a look around. She apparently was looking for fleas and head lice, so we were all told. Fancy telling kids that, a red rag to a bull that was for sure. We started going around picking on the younger kids, grabbing their hair and throwing imaginary fleas at them. Crikey! I had never seen kids run so fast in my life, they were quicker than me, and that was saying something, as long as I was not having an asthma attack.

TB (tuberculosis disease on the lungs) was rife in those days so inoculation against it had to be administered by the nurse, a 'bloody' great needle with about six prongs on it. All the kids were going behind a curtain and coming out crying. I thought here we go again; I am not going to look forward to this. But when it was my turn the nurse said I was lucky and I didn't need it because I was immune to this particular disease. What a relief, I was such a happy Bunny.

There was a rumour going around the school about a fight after school in a nearby field between the school bully and a nice guy called Frank. Apparently the bully (can't remember his name, but probably called *Coote*) had beaten Frank's younger brother up and this was revenge by him.

After school we all congregated over the field where the bully was waiting. I couldn't believe what he was holding, a bicycle chain and knuckle dusters on his fingers. There was a lot of noise, like a scene from the movies with all the kids shouting and then Frank turned up. No weapons just him, and the shouting got even louder. I thought this will be a massacre and that Frank doesn't stand a chance. How wrong was I?

The fight lasted about 15 minutes and Frank was bleeding quite badly from the effects of the chain hitting him. When eventually he managed to pull the chain away from the bully and tossed it aside. Wow! He laid in to that bully with his fists, until he was totally exhausted. The bully was finished and he held his hands up in surrender mode. Frank walked away with cheers ringing all around, just another memory, which has lasted to this day.

Ma and Pa had now decided that my school report for maths and english was not very good, so they embarked on a mission to find me a private tutor. They had this grand idea that if I had extra lessons then maybe, just maybe I might pass my 13 plus exam and could then go on to a grammar school. They certainly gave me more attention than my brother and sisters that's for sure, attention that I didn't want. What they had in mind was for me to attend a grammar school in Ilford. I was petrified; a new school was not on my agenda.

Eventually they hired a teacher to come twice a week, for two hours a night. I just don't know how they could afford it, but they did. They certainly wanted me to get on and have a future, so I shouldn't complain really. 'Must have a trade, must have trade'.................. if I heard this once, I heard it a thousand times.

I was looking out of the front window and dreading this first encounter with my new part time teacher. Around the corner came this three wheeled car with a canvas roof, spluttering and coughing as it pulled up outside, smoke bellowing out of the exhaust. It was a dreadful day weather wise, raining *'cats and dogs',* when the car door open and this tall elegant man stepped out, I thought oh jeez here we go. He rang the bell and my mother opened the door for him. 'Hello Mrs Ryder and this is Peter I presume? yes! and I hope you can prepare him for the 13 plus exams so that the little blighter has a career'.

'I'll certainly try 'was his response.

His trousers were soaking wet and my mother asked him about it. 'Oh' he said 'I have a problem with the car floor, full of holes, the water keeps splashing up.'

Funny, the things you remember.

He lasted about six weeks; I certainly was not going to show him how bright I really was. He would only recommend that damn school to my parents and I was not going to go there!

Finally my parents agreed and that was that, back to normal and back to my old school thank goodness. It was not a total waste of money; at least I did learn something.

Chapter 10
The summer of 1958

My thirteenth birthday approaches. Now I can legally apply for a paper round and get paid for it. I approached the local newsagents in Rainham, where Harry had a job; he was eight months older than me.

About ten minutes away on my bike. I used to cycle up 3rd Avenue, through Beam Bridge school and on to the A13 where Jones' newsagent was. Fourteen bob a week, for a morning round. Fortunately I started work in the school holidays, so getting up at 6 am cycling to the newsagents and delivering the papers around the estate where I lived was a bit daunting at first. It used to take me about an hour, the bag was heavy and by the end I was knackered. Soon as I finished it was back home and straight back to bed.

As I was a willing and hardworking lad, Mr Jones asked if I would deliver evening papers to the Dagenham TB Hospital. This was about ten minutes to cycle, and I had to see a Nurse *Ryley,* when I arrived at the hospital.

'Hello young man, just leave the papers here' he was a male nurse. Completely threw me, I had only had experiences with female nurses when I was at Great Ormond Street Hospital. He was completely 'MAD'. He would run around the nurses living accommodation completely 'starker's', scaring the daylights out of all the other female nurses. I just couldn't believe it, what was a matter with him, why did he behave like this.................

Eventually he was reported and he did start to behave in a more gentlemanly manner. After the initial scaremongering that he gave me, I did like to see him. He would tell loads of jokes in his Irish accent, and I started to warm to him and eventually would look forward to delivering the papers. Great fun!

I started job moonlighting. On Saturday evenings I would go to the Princess Parade and there would be a 'News' seller, selling the Saturday classified news. These papers would have all the latest football results and was very popular. So I asked him if I could help out and sell some papers for him.

'Sure you can son. But I want you to walk around the streets shouting *Star, News, Standard* at the top of your voice, and for every prior you sell I will give you a shilling'.

'What's a prior' I said

'Twenty newspapers' he said

'OK Mister' so off I went to sell newspapers.

Crikey! It was hard, *Star, News Standard* I shouted at the top of my voice. Nobody would come out of their houses to buy the papers. *The Evening Star, News or Standard.* So I thought I've had enough of this. I started to knock on the doors and guess what! I started to sell newspapers. Another lesson learnt, and a few bob earned.

Back to my morning round and Mr Jones asked if I could get to the shop for about 05.30 am. He wanted help to push his mobile shed across the A13, so that the Ford Foundry workers would stop and buy their papers and cigarettes from him. He wasn't going to pay me any extra money to do this. But I saw an opportunity here.

As we trundled across the road and parked the shed on the pavement I had the chance of pinching a couple of packs of cigs.

He never noticed me helping myself, so this was a start of further entrepreneurial activities for me.

The problem of coarse with this, was that I had to hide my contraband, couldn't take the cigs home my Mum would kill me. So I grabbed an old cigar tin from my Dad's drawer at home, put the cigs in and then buried it in the alley not far from where I lived, but on the way to school. This was my buried treasure. I would ask around at school with the other kids, to see who would buy some cigs off me. I soon became very popular. Demand far outstripped my supplies, so getting up at 05.30 am was now becoming a necessity. With orders for *Senior Service and Rothmans* the most popular.

There was always one, 'got any Dominoes' one kid asked.

'No I can't get those' I said 'you will have to buy them at the Tuck shop'. These were a pack of four small cigs that were becoming popular with the kids. The people in the Tuck shop always sold them to the kids without questions being asked.

We would sometimes go roller skating at the Ilford Roller dome, usually on a Saturday. This activity at least kept us off the streets for a while, until I got beaten up by some older boys. I was minding my own business standing at the bus stop, when a gang came up to me and started shouting about how I kept skating in to them, and of course I said it must have been somebody else, nothing to do with me. This bigger kid kept on and on 'Ginger I know it was you' and with that he punched me, knocked me to the ground and then started kicking. I burst out crying and tried to avoid his kicks. He was much bigger than our little gang and so was his gang. There were a few older people waiting for the bus, but they just ignored what was going on. I was now bleeding badly from my face, when suddenly he stopped. Some stranger had come over and lashed in to him. He fell to the ground, then got up quickly and started to run shouting back at me 'you're dead Ginger if you ever come back here'. The stranger helped me up and made sure I was OK, and then had a go at all the other people at the bus stop for not doing anything about it...

'This kid is about five years younger than that mob that attacked him. I can't believe you all allowed this to happen' with that he left and I felt so grateful that I could still walk. The bus came, so it was time to go home. I never went roller skating again for quite some time after that incident.

When I got home as usual, Ma wanted to give me another hiding for getting in to trouble. I just couldn't win, 'wasn't my fault I said'

Chapter 11

'Arthur, where shall we go today'?

I dunno, you tell me,

'Well!' I said, 'what if we get a bus to Matchstick Island and get a boat out, it's such a nice day' so that's what we did. This was a place near Becontree.

Only trouble was, when we got there, they only had sailing dinghies. We had Jimmy with us, a bit younger than Arthur and me, so the three of us hired this dingy for an hour. Didn't know how to sail it, but thought this will be a laugh.

The wind picked up, 'Jimmy, hold that rope' I shouted, but he let go and the boom hit him in the midriff and he went flying over into the water. Arthur and I raced over to try and get him out. That was a big mistake. The dingy toppled over and we all fell out, with the dingy on top of us. Talk about panic, we were so scared we thought we were all going to drown. Then Jimmy stood up. The water came up to his chest and for me and Arthur to our hips. Fortunately the island was just a short wade away and we managed to get there and started to shout as loud as we could. As there were other boats out there a man eventually came to rescue us. Got back to the mainland, got told off and just laid around until we were dry.

What a laugh, great fun and another experience to cherish.

Like all kids we all enjoyed the fun of the Fair. The fairground was here again at the local park. So with our saved up pocket money we ventured over to have a few hours on the rides'. One had to avoid the bullies; otherwise they would nick our hard earned shillings.

The Big Wheel, the Caterpillar and Ghost trains were the favourites, with the sounds of the *Everly brothers* and *Johnny kid and the Pirates* to keep us all happy at the Fair. We would have the usual fights with other kids just to make the day of it. Then run away to fight another day

The caterpillar ride was the real favourite. We use to wait until the girls got on board, and then me an Arthur would rush on next to them. As the ride started to move the cover came over the top of us and the centrifugal force would push us on to the girls. Screaming and shouting the girls loved it.

The Rebel   **Milky Bar Kid**

Sunday nights at home could be so boring unless of course Uncle Wal and Doris turned up. They would always arrive unexpectedly just in time for tea. Ma would moan and groan about it, but it was her older brother and they lived in Kent. So they would drive over and get a free meal. Ma would open her best tin of '*John West red salmon*' and we would all sit around the table with our salmon salads and tin of ham, followed by the Winkles and Cockles that we used to get off the wheel-barrow man in the street doing his rounds.

After our hearty tea we would all settle down and play cards and that included me this time. We used to play for money, pennies and a few bob. The games would include *sevens or nomination whist*. So with my hard earned pocket money I would play and try to earn a few more shillings. Guest what? I would always win.

'You little bugger' my Aunt Doris would always say this, just because I would win.

'I don't know how you do it' she would shout

'You're a little cheat' she would keep on saying. I said to her if I was really the milky bar kid and was accused like that, I would shoot you. She would just laugh. This was the time when a commercial came on TV advertising milky bars. A kid that looked like me with freckles was the hero, the '*Milky bar Kid',* was coming to town I started becoming known as this kid. Wow! How great that made me feel.

Back at school and time for the music class. The worst two lessons at school were music and religious studies. Oh, how we all hated those lessons. We would all attend the classes but they became a 'free for all'. The teachers were always women and they could not control us. We were so noisy, shouting and throwing books until finally I would pick up the ink well that was on my table and throw it at some kid I didn't like. Oh dear! gone too far this time. Teacher grabbed me by the ear and escorted me out of the class, and I was told to wait there until the Headmaster did his rounds along the corridor. That was bad news, really bad, for I knew what would be coming next. There was a deathly silence in the corridor, and I was sweating profusely, when around the corner the headmaster started his approach.

'Boy! follow me to my quarters'.....................everyone was petrified of the headmaster. His powers were supreme. He could expel you or just administer punishment, whichever he thought was appropriate to the crime.

'So boy, why were you outside your music room' he shouted.

'Well Sir' I tried to explain that I was wrongly accused but he was not having any of that.

'What hand do you hold the pencil with' he now calmly spoke.

'Sir, the right hand' that was a mistake I should have said the left, then I couldn't have done any work for the rest of the day.

'Hold your left hand out boy' and with that he brought the cane out and hit me ten times on the fingers. Owchhhhhhhhhh! That really hurt, my fingers didn't stop hurting for hours.

'Now get back to your classroom and tell Miss Cramphorn I have dealt with you, and if I see you again this week your punishment will be very severe'.

After that I did try not to get in to trouble again, but it was difficult.

There were times when we had 'PE'; I would be suffering from an asthma attack.

I had to have a note from my Ma to excuse me from this vigorous exercise, otherwise the attacks would just get worst and I would need to see the Doctor.

We would all have to go out and run across country tracks in the heart of midwinter in just our shorts and vest. I hated to do that. So eventually I would have a note every time we had to do this. However me being me, I would write it out myself. I used to get away with it for some time, until the teacher caught on. Then when he did he made me go out longer. I eventually told Ma and she came to the school had a go at the 'Ogre' of a teacher and finally I was relieved of any more running exercises. What a relief, so now it was just the rope climbing, bench jumps and any other torture that he could think of.

In the sports programme was obviously, football. I was average at this but on occasions we would have to have a heading competition. I used to be pretty good, heading the ball much further than any of the other kids, so that again made me popular. When choosing the sides the captains would like me in defence, so at least I was not the last embarrassed kid to be picked.

This was also the year when my parents paid for another school trip. This time kids from our year, the ones that could afford it were going on a holiday to Belgium. *Blankenburg* was the town, close to the beach, had a great time there. The promenade had a place where you could hire unusual cycles. They were called crazy bikes, all different shapes and sizes. Bent frames, one wheel bikes, four seater's, the list could go on. We stayed at a small hotel about thirty of us, and once again the noise was deafening. Teachers had no control over us; we were very rowdy and used to steal anything. On one occasion the Chinese Chef would run us out of the hotel, because of some kids going into the kitchen, stealing food and pelting it at him. He would chase us down the road waving a meat cleaver in his hand, bloody maniac.

We all had a day out by coach to see the **Atomium** in Brussels. This had just been built this year. The **Atomium** is a monument in Brussels, originally built for Expo '58, the 1958 Brussels World's Fair, and it stands 102 metres (335 ft.) high.
This monument represented an atom, and at the time was fascinating. We all went inside, each silver ball was linked with escalators and in each ball there would be an exhibition of some sorts, but I can't remember the details.

The Atomium

On another day out we had a coach ride across the border to Holland. A small town near the city of Amsterdam. The coach parked in the main square which was also close to a river. Thirty kids jumped off even before the teachers could control us. They shouted at us to be back in one hour as we ran across the square and headed for the first tourist shop. What 'mayhem'. We all ran into this shop and literally raided it, taking anything we could grab. We then all scarpered as quick as our little feet would carry us, all in different directions, as the poor owner came racing out trying to catch some of us, but to no avail.

I grabbed a large cuddly dog and a wallet, plus a few other little things that I could put in my pocket.

That one hour went very quick. My mate at the time was Jack; the two of us were now walking back by the river heading for the coach, when in the distance we could see police cars and a lot of police.

"Jack, do you see what I see?

Bloody hell, what we gonna do, the police are at our Coach, we are all gonna get arrested, and carted off to prison.

Not if we throw away our contraband" I said. So I immediately threw it into the river my cuddly dog and all the gear I had in my pockets. Jack did the same.

But I kept the wallet. It was too nice to throw away. Leather, with a picture of Holland on the face, I wasn't going to throw that away. So I took my shoe off and shoved it down my sock and put my shoe back on again. Marched up to the coach, said hello to the Police and got back on.

"Ok you lot, what have you been up too?" said the teacher. "The Police want you all off this coach and to line up outside, turn out your pockets for inspection. A shop was raided not far from here by a gang of English children, and they are searching everyone who might be involved. It better not be any of you, because this is really serious and they will arrest you"

I thought to myself, hope we don't have to take our shoes and socks off as well.

Phew! We got the all clear, everyone was smart. The Police moved on to another coach and we all got on board and headed back to our Hotel. What a day and I still had my wallet.

I thought; better not go home without a present for my mum. So I actually went along to a shop and bought her a gift. It was a small figurine of a porcelain lamb, all boxed up and tied with a beautiful bow. She loved it and to this day I still have it, still in one piece, made in Japan. We called it 'Bambi', another lasting memory, of that school holiday.

Top Photo – Me and Rocky in our back garden

Lower Photo – Me on a Mountain. Austria 1959

Top Photo – Ma and Pa Seefeld Austria

Lower Photo – Ma and Me in Belgium

Maggi, Eileen, Aunt Doris and Ma

My Two Wonderful Sisters (1953)

Maggi – Territory Army

94 Red

Bambi

Uncle Albert – War Hero

Killed in Burma 1943

(Photo taken 1940 aged 18)

96 Red

Granma playing the *ivories* her 90th Birthday

Chapter 12

Cycling Adventures

Reggie and I started to become good mates. We both had our nice bikes and would often go on a cycling trip to Canvey Island or Brighton and also to Saffron Waldon. We joined the Youth Hostel Association (YHA). Ma and Pa paid the fee and gave me money to spend the night in the Hostel. It used to be about two bob for a night and for this you would get a bed in a dormitory with loads of other youths. You had to fend for yourself, cook your own breakfast and make your own drinks. Although for a small fee the warden would prepare a small meal for you at dinner time. It's hard to believe now that our parents were quite happy for us to go away on our own. We couldn't keep in contact for we had no phone at home. If you phoned from one of those red GPO phone kiosks you always had to press button A or B to get through, anyway as no one had a phone it didn't matter.

I volunteered one morning to cook bacon and eggs, when all of a sudden the frying pan caught alight.

'Reggie put it out?' I shouted, but the Warden was on hand to extinguish it for me. At least we didn't burn the Hostel down

On another occasion we started to cycle to Southend. We had our tent with us and decided we would do a bit of camping. We had cycled for about 2 hours and it was getting late. We saw a field, well there were loads of them and so decided to camp overnight. We had no food or water just a few sweets. Erected our small tent and got ready for the night. It was getting dark and scary now! We were getting second thoughts about this, but it was now too late to change our minds.

'Did you hear that Pete' (My real mates called me by my real name) cried out Reggie

'Hear what?' I said

'That bloody scary noise' he shouted

Mooooooo!.... mooooo!.....moooo!, and then there was a silhouette reflecting on the tent canvass. It started to shuffle on the side of the tent. I thought blow this I'm going to run for it. 'Come on Reggie lets un-zip and bolt.

'Helpppppppp...............' we shouted as we ran towards the nearby road, looking back when we were far enough away. We both stumbled and fell over into a 'Cow pack'.

It was a bloody heard of Cows'. Wow! We were so relieved. As they started to walk away we managed to go back and collect all of our belongings. That was enough for today, and it was only 6 am. It was now time to go home and get some breakfast.

Chapter 13

Another Summer Holiday 1958

The summer school holidays seemed to last forever. When the weather was good Arthur and me used to cycle to the Chase Romford, where we could scrub out the horses stables and scrounge a ride late in the day.

There was always one kid who didn't want to do this, but still get a free ride on a horse. He was bloody horrible. He kept spitting at the rest of us kids. He was much bigger, so no one would take him on for a fight. We would all sit on the hay in one of the open stables until the stable owner chose some of us to ride a horse for a one hour ride. We could all ride a bit, had lessons at these stables. Some free and some paid by our parents. I chose my horse and three other kids got to choose theirs. Including the horrible one, Mick was his name.

We were out in the open fields cantering over the meadow and into the woods, what great fun this was. I felt as if I was a real Cowboy riding to the 'Bonanza' ranch in some American film. Arthur was right behind me and we used to race each other when 'Wack' I came flying off. Catapulted in to the air and fell hard to the ground. Arthur behind just missed me on his horse. A tree branch got in my way, I couldn't duck my head quick enough. Took all the wind out my body but I was alright, I'll live to ride another day. My horse just bolted back to the stables, so Arthur gave me a ride back.

The good news when we returned was that Mick also came off his horse and wasn't so lucky, broke his leg............oh! How we all laughed, didn't see him again, that summer.

On those terrible wet days when I couldn't go out I would spend most of my time drawing and painting. It would always be a character out of my comics. Some were really good and I would enter them into competitions. Now and again I would win a stupid prize. I only wish my mother had not thrown them away when I was older. She did have a habit like that..........throw it out, throw it out. Another part of my child legacy dumped.

Ma and Pa took me on another week's holiday this time to Butlins in Phewelli Wales. We met a mate of my Pa there and spent a lot of time with them. They had a daughter and for the first time I had a crush on a young lady, however my shyness was always going to be a problem. It was never going to be any more than that.

They lived somewhere in Forest Gate, so when we arrived home and on the following week I would cycle to their house. I never called at their door but just kept cycling around where they lived, to try and get the courage to knock on their front door. I was cycling along one of the paths when all of a sudden Jeannie and her mum were heading towards me – no escape, I was caught.

'What are you doing here Peter? You're a long way from home, does your mother know' Jeannie's mother shouted. And of course I was embarrassed like hell. 'Dunno really' I said, 'thought I would just go for a ride'

'Well come on round to our house and I'll make you a nice cup of tea'.

So that was it really. Cycled over every day just to see 'Jeannie' during the summer holidays.

Pressure was really on me now to find some more fags for the kids at school. One particular day I turned up at the paper shop to do my round as usual and was told by Mrs Jones that the cellar was flooded and could I come back later and help to clear up the mess, there had been a lot of rain that week. She offered me some extra money so obviously I could not refuse.

The cellar was about three feet deep in water, so my mission was to salvage as much of the stock that I could. The cellar had a couple of these small high windows to the back and I thought what an opportunity here. I managed to slide out the windows a couple of hundred fags to collect later when I was finished down here. 'Worked a treat'. I went back upstairs and they were very pleased with my help, even gave me a sweet for my troubles. Went around the back and put my contraband in my news bag then I was off, a new supply for the kids back at school. On the way back I went via the alley and stored them in my cigar box until I returned to school.

'Hello boy, what's your name' I met this huge dog in my street, he was just wandering around and he had a name tag on his collar, 'ROCKY' was his name. I immediately took to him and him to me. He followed me home and I gave him some food. He was wonderful, played with him in my garden. He was now my friend for life. We would go on many adventures together. He even helped me with my paper round, mornings and nights. It took me a while to find out where Rocky lived. He would stay with me most of the day and at tea time would suddenly disappear. On one evening I followed him. He lived just a block away. There was this big six foot gate to his garden and he would just leap over it to get in. So now I knew. When I wanted him I would go around there and whistle. He would come, cantering like a horse full speed and jump over the gate. He became my friend for many years, even when eventually I had a full time job in London.

When I did my Sunday morning paper round, Rocky would always be with me even in those dark winter mornings. I used to hang a bag with a few newspapers in it around his head and we would both march off happily whistling to the latest pop songs of the week.

Now and again the weather got very hot, so it was fortunate that just a short walk away was *Leys swimming baths.* Jimmy, Arthur and me would go to the pool for the day. One had to get there early due to the massive queues to get in. Once inside we had to find our pitch, which was at the north end of the pool on a small hill of grass. You just could not move. Seemed like thousands of kids were here, ready to cool off. Nobody bothered about sun cream; it just was not around at the time. Being a ginger haired kid I was more prone than others for getting sunburnt, but that was the least of my troubles, I couldn't swim. Petrified to go in the deep end, so would play in the three feet end, just to be safe. But today that was all going to change. Some bigger kids from my school recognised me, the ones who didn't regularly get their fags quota from me. They grabbed hold of me and dragged me to the middle of the side of the pool, the deep end and threw me in. How I missed the concrete edge, I just don't know. Down and down I went, coughing and spluttering. I thought I was going to drown................... Then somebody grabbed hold of me and pulled me to the surface. It was the lifeguard!

I was alright, didn't have to get me into the recovery position, but he got hold of the kids that threw me in and banished them from the pool. Phew! That did shake me up. But I promised myself no more. I got back in and doggy paddled until eventually got the confidence to go in the deep end of the pool.

From there on I started swimming regularly and would often go over to the pool on my own. Jumping off the ten metre board and diving from the three meter board. What a difference and all because some kids threw me in.

Unfortunately when I got home my mother had another go at me.

'Look at yourself, your full of blisters' and I was. It was really hurting, so my mother covered me in 'calamine lotion' to cool me down. It didn't teach me anything, couldn't go swimming with a shirt on. I would be called a bloody Sissy.

Ma – In Surprise Mood

Pa – Usual Pose at His Garden Shed

Chapter 14

Back to School 3rd year

So it was back to school again. New lessons, other than the maths and English of course! After assembly we reported back to Mr Lions again and received the new curriculum for this term. Included this year was Technical drawing, Metalwork, Woodwork and Art, I enjoyed them all. I think this was the year when I now started to show some interest in my lessons and the beginnings of something new.

There was a new craze in the playgrounds this year. Down by the bike shed we would grab hold of the younger kids and get them to cross over their legs around the shed roof supports. They would then have to sit down, and with their legs crossed couldn't pull themselves up. What a laugh, really funny. Then when the bell rang to go back to our classes, we would leave them out there. It was only when we had to move on to the next lesson, when the register was called that the teachers realised what had happened. Crikey did we get a roasting for that. Nobody would own up. However when we attended the sports masters class, a Mr Biggs (large man with a big temper to match) he would sought out the culprits and get them to bend over a chair where he would administer 10 hits with his favourite shoe over our *backsides*. If we had time the savvy kids would push a comic inside there trousers to take out the sting, but you did have to be quick without him noticing, otherwise it would be twenty hits if he discovered this little ploy.

I used to go home for my lunch and make myself a sandwich, generally 'pan-yan pickle' and *Rocky* would sometimes be waiting for me, outside the back gate. I'd make him one as well, until my 'bloody' brother would also come home from work and have a moan at me for feeding him. Use to give me a bit of a slap for my troubles. Mother would be working at the butchers so she wasn't there. Anyway, on my return back to school I would go via the ditch that ran from *Rainham* to *Ballard's* road and play at jumping across it with Rocky.

I was in class in the afternoon when the headmaster came looking for me.

'Ryder' he called 'there is a large animal stalking the corridors and I have been informed that he belongs to you'

'No Sir, he doesn't, but I know where he lives'

'Well! Take him home, I don't want him unsettling the rest of the school'. With that he left and so I grabbed hold of Rocky and we both marched off and headed back to the ditch and happily played for the rest of the afternoon.

From then on when there was a lesson that I didn't like, I would always take *Rocky* with me. What a whizz, it worked every time.

Rocky

Rocky (with my attempt at hand colouring the photo)

108 Red

Eventually I arrived home from my afternoon out with Rocky. Dad was sitting at the table doing his accounts for the 'Mill house' Social Club. Apparently he was there treasurer and he did this in his spare time. I thought imagine that, adding all those figures up for no pay. I guess he must be pretty intelligent to do that. He did use to help me with my maths homework, so that was a help.

I remember asking him, when I plucked up the courage, 'what did you do in the war Dad'?

He looked at me with a puzzled look, as if to say mind your own bloody business, 'you are just a kid', and then thought differently about it. Due to ill health he was never conscripted to join the armed forces. So he became the Air Raid Warden for our street. Had to make sure the blackouts were in force in all the neighbours windows and to make sure when the sirens sounded that they all rushed into their air raid shelters. Ours was in the back garden *'Anderson shelter'* I thought that was cool.

I asked my Mother what was Dad's ill health during the war. She said something about his feet being to flat. 'What! I didn't understand that. Everyone had flat feet. Otherwise we wouldn't be able to walk. Anyway I left it at that, too complicated for a kid.

She did say however that towards the end of the war 'Old Hitler' sent these pilotless planes over to bomb the stuffing out of us and to inflict as much damage on the Fords foundry. *Doodlebugs* they were called and one actually landed near the Mill House, blew out the windows of peoples' houses all around. I suppose that was where I used to play, on the old bombsites.

September was a happy time. My sister Iris had a baby, what joyous times these were. Gary was his name and the first born in the Ryder family. Ma and me would often go over to see him and hold and cuddle him. She really did gloat on him and I suppose I did as well. Buying him loads of presents and as he got older Ma would give away most of my toys to him. I didn't mind at the time, until I got older myself and realised my childhood material history was disappearing.

Christmas was approaching again, so it was time to think of the presents for Ma and Pa to buy me again..............the days of believing in Father Christmas were now long gone. What a great feeling it used to be, believing in Father Christmas, with the build-up and the excitement of going to bed and waking up with a sack full of presents.

Pa would leave a mince pie and a glass of milk on the table at the bottom of my bed. In the morning it was gone and Wow! That really was great, to think he came in to my room and to all the rooms of the children around the world, Magical! I would always try to stay awake on Christmas Eve just to see him, but of course it wasn't to be, eventually falling to sleep and dreaming of wondrous things to come.

This year I had a train set as my main present (Hornby) fantastic. Set it up in the front room as soon as I was up. This was one of the best Christmases of my young life so far. Iris and family, Maggi and my brother were all here for the day.

After the presents were opened, Pa played his classical music in the background, Ma, cooking away, fantastic. It really was good, no arguments and everyone getting along just fine

I used to still get up at 5 am to do my paper round. Trudge to the newspaper shop and collect my papers to deliver. Because I was always early the few people that did, left me an envelope of tips attached to their doorknocker, at this time of the year, very rewarding. I was getting a bit of a hoarder at saving money now. Rocky was up early as well and giving me a helping paw. I would complete it within an hour and then it was straight back to bed. Rocky would stay around until I got up again.

Back at school and I was now slowly becoming a conscientious scholar. I was now taking an interest in most lessons, but especially technical drawing. We were all given a small drawing board with a T square. The subject would be a spanner and we would have to draw this in a three dimensional scale. There would be many items as the lessons progressed and I seemed to be rather good at it. Unknowingly this part of my schooling was going to influence my whole career for the future

I joined a youth club at the Co-Operative hall in the New Year, for something to do in those long winter nights. I used to go twice a week with Arthur. We would do the usual stuff like running, playing British bulldog, boxing and a whole host of other in-door sports to keep warm. There was never any heating inside. So with swapping comics, selling fags, running amok under the moonlight over the local field, this was my winter occupation.

Summer was approaching again thank goodness. And so were the end of term exams. Ma and Pa had now booked a holiday to Austria, Seefeld. Hadn't a clue where it was except that we were to go on a coach, on a Ferry, drive through Holland, Belgium, Germany and finally arriving at Seefeld two days later. All this was to happen in August. I must admit I was a bit apprehensive about this, because as usual there would be no kids for me to play with again and I would be bored stiff again.

Before all this there was still the adventures' of Barking Park and rowing on the boats. Arthur and me would hire out these 'one man skips', I think that is what you call them. The seats would roll back and forwards with the motion of our rowing and we would race up and down the lake finishing off with going to the Fair within the park. This was a regular event on Saturdays and great fun.

My brother had purchased a motor bike this year. A 500cc Norton, bloody powerful thing and he would sometimes put me on the pinion seat and take me to Southend. Blimey, the speed he travelled at was like lightning. We arrived at our destination and would immediately go over to the seafood hut and have some *jellied eels,* the highlight of our journey. After that it was over to the racetrack next to the Pier for five laps around the track.

For some reason my brother was beginning to like me, I think!, and taking me for rides on his bike. He now would often take me to see West Ham United play, as I was now interested in football, especially after the Manchester United air crash. So I suppose he wasn't all that bad after all.

Chapter 15

The summer of 1959

Another birthday June 11th 1959, fourteen years old and still the *'cheeky chappie',* so I am told.

So now it was time for our holiday to Austria. I think my Pa booked this holiday with his social club at Fords. The coached picked us up at the Mill house at 6 am and we were on our way. We had two drivers on the coach one slept while the other one drove. The coach only stopped for comfort breaks until we arrived in a small town in West Germany where we all stayed for the night. No dinner, just a snack and straight to bed. Breakfast was awful, dried bread and cold meats', I surely missed my cereals for breakfast. Back on the coach 6 am again and departed for our final destination. I was tired and slept most of the way. Finally we arrived, In Seefeld, early evening. It was idyllic just like a picture postcard, what a beautiful town. All the houses and hotels appeared to be set in a time warp; I never forgot that experience to this day. The mountains, snow capped with beautiful lakes in the valleys, absolutely amazing.

Obviously I had to share the room with my parents, but that was alright, didn't know any better and the fact that the bathroom was down the corridor was just like home really, not downstairs.

There was no swimming pool, so that peeved me off a bit, until I was told that if I walked a mile up through the pass, there was a lake I could swim in. I thought great that will do me.

The next day I left my Ma and Pa and marched up to the lake. Couldn't get lost, lots of people were doing exactly the same.

I settled down with my towel and thought here goes, let's swim. I got about one third of the way and realised I was not going to make it. The water was freezing and I was slowing down. I started to shout for help but nobody else was swimming and they couldn't hear me at the edge of the lake. I thought *'oh Jesus'* what am I going to do? Don't panic, don't panic I kept saying to myself. I tried to float but it was too cold for that. I saw the shortest route back and started out for it. I swam faster even though I was tired for a further ten minutes, until eventually, out of breath and exhausted I tried to tread water but to my relief my feet touched the muddy bottom and Phew! I could relax a bit. It was still another ten minutes before I got back to dry land with my feet and legs caked in mud.

Never again, they say you learn by your mistakes. I certainly did that day and fortunately survived it.

I never told Ma and Pa. Pa would probably understand but my mother would have shouted at me so loud that she would have probably caused an avalanche and that was something I didn't want to see.

Other than that experience I had a great time in Seefeld. Had a trip to Innsbruck on the mountain train and loads of mountain walks.

I bought myself a nice Tyrolean hat at the local tourist shop; it had a feather inserted one side of the hat. I thought I looked brilliant and couldn't stop wearing it, but in reality I probably looked like a twerp. I would walk around the streets and mountain valleys, *yodelling!* This was well before *Del Shannon* came out with his worldwide hit *'The Swiss Maid'*, which I immediately bought when it was released.

Towards the end of the holiday I still had some money left, so I waited until we were all packed and ready to go and told my Ma that I was just going down to the shop to buy a present for Arthur. I bought 200 fags but to get them all the way home without Ma and Pa finding out I had to be clever. So I un-wrapped the carton and put the packets under my shirt around my waste. I did look a bit fat but fortunately no one noticed. The coach travelled all the way home with just three stops, no hotels this time. The problem was of course getting through customs. My Pa was fully loaded up with his pipe tobacco and fags for his mates at work, so if they searched me he would probably be in for a lot of trouble. But they didn't, after all I was just a kid, why would they?

Safely home, with my hoard of contraband. It was straight to my alley where I put them in my box ready to sell on when it was back to school time.

I discovered when I got home that my brother had now bought an air rifle. That was a big mistake, by him. We would practice firing at target cards in the garden and got pretty good at it. He used to store it in the wardrobe of his bedroom; we both had our own bedrooms, now that the Sisters' had moved out. Once again I was tempted to be mischievous. I would put some bread out at the bottom of the garden and climb up the clothes line post and leave some bread there, on the top. Get the gun and go into my Ma and Pa's bedroom, open the window and wait patiently for the birds to arrive. They were always *sparrows*, I think. Took aim and fired. Didn't shoot many really, but those that were killed I had to bury them. Not really proud of that episode in my young life, that's for sure. Even took the rifle over the local wasteland for shooting practice. The other kids thought it was great and so did I. What a very bad lad.

Chapter 16

Back to school 4th and Final year

So here we are, my final year at Marley Secondary School for boys'. The pressure is on to study really hard this year. The rest of my life will depend on it, so said all the teachers and my parents, I guess I did as well, never thought at this time what I wanted to do when I left school. That would not really hit me until the spring of next year. At least now the technical drawing was the biggest influence on me, but what good was that, I didn't know at the time.

We had a new Art teacher at school and he had quite a macabre imagination. We kids would have to draw unusual creatures escaping or climbing out of square holes from the ground. The scariest and the most frightening drawings got the highest marks. I loved it! I excelled in this class, with my drawings from the creepy underworld. My imagination ran away with me. I never took *Rocky* to school when attending these classes.

I stayed in the 'A' form throughout my days at Marley, so that gave me some confidence. From being 40th in a class of 44 to achieving mid 20's was a result for me. At least I improved over the years much to the satisfaction of my parents.

There were still a few mishaps in the classroom, however. Mr Lions would leave the room and of course we kids would never be quiet. On one occasion when the milk bottle boy brought the crate of milk into the classroom, everyone would race to try and get two bottles. Fights broke out and bottles were dropped and smashed to the ground. One kid I remember to this day 'Briggsy' was his name, picked up a broken bottle and playfully lashed out at some of us. Unfortunately he struck me and cut my left thumb.

Blood was gushing out everywhere. At that moment Mr Lions returned...............suddenly you could have heard a pin drop, he shouted, 'Get back to your seats the lot of you', I passed out for a few seconds, well I would wouldn't I?.

Mr Lions was looking at me when I came too.

'How are you feeling Ryder'?

'I don't know Sir'

'James take him to first aid and get that thumb looked at'

'Yes sir, I'm on my way' James replied

When we got back everyone in the class had got one smack of the cane across their hand, administered by Mr Lions. James and I were also given one later, when he felt I was well enough. I thought we were going to get away with it, but it wasn't to be.

We all had detention for an hour after school and had to write five hundred lines of............'.I am naughty, must behave in class from now on'. But of course we didn't, nothing ever changes. I still have that scar on my thumb to this day.

My brother was clever. He had made a tape recorder, one of the first I could ever recall. It had those reels made of tape and a microphone, so that you could record yourself on. He had also bought a clarinet and practised Dave Brubeck tunes to playback and listen to. I thought he sounded crap and told him so. Wack! That wasn't a good idea as he hit me on the head with his clammy hand. Anyway this would be about the time I began to listen to pop music, even though it was difficult. There was only the BBC radio and they didn't play much popular music at the time. Ma and Pa bought me a transistor radio. This was the first type of a personal music player. It was small and obviously all the rage with our generation. So around about 10.30 on a Sunday night you could listen to the latest music being played at that time, Not a very good reception but I would go to bed with my radio and plug the earpiece into my good ear. David Jacob's I think was the *DJ,* playing the pick of the pops for the week on radio Luxemburg. I would fall asleep and the bloody batteries would run out of power. *Elvis, Cliff* and my favourites would be *Roy Orbison* and *Adam Faith.* This was the start of a singing career, or so I thought. I would play my Adam Faith record on my Dads' HMV Black Box stereo music station and over sing *Adam* whilst taping at the same time. I sounded crap as well, let alone my brother. I wouldn't give up though. I practised and practiced until eventually I really sounded.............gr...t. No! I never improved, I had a lousy voice but it kept me busy and I did enjoy trying to improve myself but it wasn't to be. No *X factor* fame for me. *Sandy Shaw, Max Bygraves, Dudley Moore* and not forgetting the *Dagenham Girl Pipers* all became famous from Dagenham but not me.

Down at the local ABC cinema in New Road I was now getting too old to go to Saturday Morning Club. This was the time when X films would be shown. You had to be sixteen years old to get in. So I guess this was the next challenge, looking older than I was to get in and see the latest shockers of the Fifties.

The queue outside on a Sunday evening was huge. But with a little bit of 'sauce' the lady at the kiosk would let me and Arthur in. It didn't really matter what the film was, getting in was all that mattered.

'It, the Terror from Outer Space' was the first film I ever saw. And just like the TV series of the Quatermass Experiment, was just as frightening. This film did its job, frightened the life out of me. Whilst walking home with Arthur, well we ran actually, as fast as our little legs would take us, we would be looking at the hedges and thinking there were creatures in there that could eat us.

Had to tell my Ma to leave the light on that night and for a long time after that

This experience didn't stop us. We just wanted to see more. The Trollenburge Terror was another one of those films, about a mist in the Swiss Alps that turned people bonkers. Crikey, we never learnt our lesson.

Old Broad Street 1954

Leys Swimming Baths

Heathway Cinema

Chapter 17
End of Term 1960

With my exams finished it was now time to think about what I was going to do with the rest of my life. The Employment officer came to our school and individually interviewed each kid. I was still only fourteen until June. There were no extra years, I had to find a job and hopefully my employers would give me release from work to further my education.

Pa, was always at hand at this time to coax me along and give me some ideas and encouragement.

So when the Employment officer came around to see me and asked what I wanted to do I said a *Pop Singer*, no really a *Draughtsman.* That started the ball rolling. Interview with the London office of Education was arranged. It was located in the East of London near Fenchurch Street.

I thought to myself.................why can't I just play forever, I don't want to work and I certainly don't want to go to London. To me that was like a foreign country, thousands of miles away. That place was always covered in fog; just as my asthma was improving it would start to get bad again.

It was not to be. The arrangements were made and I had an appointment sometime in May.

No holidays this year, waiting for exam results and job interviews. Bloody boring! But I still had some time to play.

At the weekends over the local wasteland some brave kid had climbed up a tree, crawled out onto a branch and tied a rope. Those that could would use it as a *Tarzan* swing. We climbed on to it above the ridge and swung out over the ravine. This was really great. There would be many fights over the rites to command this piece of property. But the kid that originally did the work for this swing would eventually turn up and he was a big brute. So we minnows had to run for our lives when he appeared.

'Well are you ready son?' my Dad was going with me to London for that interview.

We got the bus from new road to Heathway and then boarded a train to London. The District line they called it. All the carriages were full of smoke.

Everyone was smoking, even my Dad. It was the norm in those days and it played havoc with my asthma................again.

Arrived at the Employment office and was introduced to another officer. He sat me and Dad down and asked me what I was interested in and of course I told him. I wanted to be a draughtsman. 'OK, 'he said 'there is an opportunity at this small engineering office in *Chancery Lane* for an apprentice draughtsman. They are looking for two. So he rang them up and made an appointment for me in about one hour's time.

Dad and I arrived at this *Dickenson* building just off *Chancery Lane*. I thought this just looks awful and it was just as bad inside the office. It was one room with an old man sitting at a desk, with another old man sitting on a stool, his back to us. He was drawing something on a gigantic drawing board. The light was bad and the smell of *Old Spice* combined with smoke and wood was everywhere. This did not impress me at all, I almost wanted to cry.

'Hello Young man, my name is *Mr Berriff, (A W)* they called him, I think that was his initials but nobody had told me, and what is your name?

'Peter, Sir,' I replied. Anyway he rambled on about the company and that they were expanding on account of so much work for the company and were looking for two young boys to employ.

He said if I was interested there were great opportunities for me in this profession. We would put you on trial for one year and when you get to sixteen years old offer you an apprenticeship for five years. I just couldn't take this in. Five years is one third of my life to date. It sounded to me like a life sentence in prison. But it was a Job, so I suppose I should be thankful for this.

'We will give you a day release programme at college to study for your certificates in structural engineering' he kept on rambling.

'But be prepared that your duties for some time will include running errands, tea making, printing, answering the phone and any other duties that may be requested by your superiors.

'I am assuming that your school exam results will be satisfactory, I have been assured by the employment agency in touch with your school that you are a good student', so Peter would you like to join *Ellis Jones and Partners.*

'Yes please Sir! I would' One had to be polite and show a good impression.

'You will be working in our other office just a short walk from here in *Furnival Street* and start after your school term finishes. So it will be at the end of July'.

He escorted me and Dad down the road to the other office. We walked up three floors to the top. *Mr Berriff* opened the door to a large office with a huge glass roof.

'Wow' that was impressive. I liked that immediately and it certainly cheered me up. There were about three old men and another office where the secretary worked. I was introduced to everyone.

'This is Peter' said *Mr Berriff*, 'and he will be joining us at the end of July. We will all be looking forward to you starting young man' said one of the other old men. Crikey there did seem a lot of old men here, but I guess it will have to be something that I will just have to get use too.

I said my goodbyes' and Dad seemed to be impressed. I didn't know how much I would be earning, didn't really care I suppose. We went for a bit of lunch at the *Lyons Corner House.* Dad treated me to see a film at the Odeon in Leicester Square called The *Seven Ancient Wonders of the World,* all in glorious cinemascope with a curved screen. Now that was, impressive, my first film in London and a blockbuster as well.

My exam results weren't great, but they weren't bad either. I mustered up about an average pass mark overall of 60%. I was ready so I thought to go out into that big bad world.

I found out later that Harry my classmate and the kid who lived up the road was working in *Chancery Lane* also. Not only that, but he was in the same profession as me. He left school at Christmas so had an early start.

A letter finally arrived in the post to confirm my start date and a grand salary of £3-10 shillings a week plus 10 shillings of luncheon vouchers. (That's £4 in todays' money). I thought that was a lot, four times my paper round money.

However by the time tax was deducted, train and bus fares plus ten bob a week to my Mother, didn't really leave me much to spend. So nothing ever changes, it's still the same today.

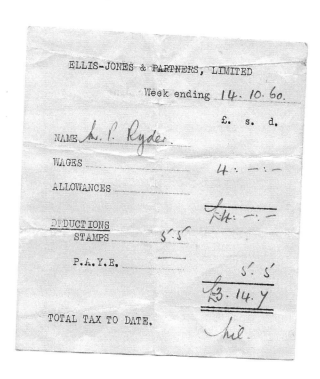

One of my First Pay Packets

We had a holiday after all. Pa had booked a caravan on a site in *Hemsby* near *Grt Yarmouth* for a week at the end of July, just before I had to start work.

The most disappointing part for me starting this new career was the amount of time I would not see *Rocky*. It would now just be weekends and I was beginning to regret this so much

Not much happened at *Hemsby*. It rained too much and once again I spent a lot of the time inside, playing the machines in the arcade.

An Earlier Photo – 11 Years Old

Chapter 18
Maggi 1937 – 1965

I have to include a few dedicated words about my beloved sister, Margaret Rose. She was always supported of me and I loved her dearly. There were eight years separating us. She was always generous to me. With pocket money and sweets and every Christmas, book me in to her factory children's' parties. She worked at *Dagenite Batteries* just off the *Chequers* corner near *Dagenham Dock.* My memories of her are sometimes blurred. She was also a smoker but tended to roll her own. She had this weird little machine that rolled the tobacco up, then she would insert a filter and Hey presto there was a fag. She did about ten in a row and then put them all in a tin. Crazy I know the things that you remember.

To me she never seemed to be quite that happy. I was only about ten or eleven when she moved out of our home. She lived in Digs on the estate for a while, then when Iris got married lived with her at *West Horndon.* Eventually she rented a flat in *Barking.*

Joined the Territorial Army where she met *Ivy* and became contented with her life. We used to wind her up about boyfriends, not bringing any home. She was obviously having some difficulties with her life but I don't think anyone in our family were aware of this.

I used to think why doesn't she come home and visit anymore. I was only a kid, so it all passed me by. In my early teens I missed her not being around and then in 1965 after being married for three months my Dad contacted me.

He was heartbroken as we all were, *Ivy,* Maggi's flat mate had died of leukaemia and the following day on New Years' Eve Maggi had taken her own life.

My brother discovered her on New Year's Day, he had a key to her flat and when he entered, it was full of carbon monoxide. He would never speak about that day ever again to anyone. Maggi had left a suicide note to my mother explaining why she had done this and to please forgive her. I still have that note.

Why Oh why? I still wonder about this sad time and think to myself, if only…….She would have grown older and I could have visited her with my children, and spent many days with her visiting me and my family. She was my Soul sister.

New years' Eve was obviously saddened forever and it didn't help that Maggi's birthday was exactly the same date as my future wife's birthday, from my mother's point of view.

My parents had her cremated at Manor Park cemetery Ilford, next to Ivy. They were her last wishes.

Your still remembered Maggi.

Maggi

Chapter 19

A New Beginning

Start my job today August 1960. What nerves, I didn't want to go, obviously. The pressure was awful and I really felt sick, but my mother almost pushed me out of the door. She gave me pocket money and sandwiches and I left home at 7 am, walked to new road bus stop about ten minutes, with a fifteen minute bus ride to Heathway station to catch the District line to London.

I didn't have to get a ticket because I had a weekly season. When I caught the train it was full of smoke. Everyone smoked and all though I didn't mind at the time, well I had spent my years selling fags so I shouldn't complain really. But in an enclosed area it would eventually affect my asthma attacks and cause me a lot of discomfort. There was only one carriage for non-smokers and that would be standing room only. I had to change at Mile End for the central line to my final destination *'Chancery Lane'.*

Arrived at *Furnival Street* early 08.45. The front door to the street was locked, so I couldn't get in. I'm standing outside like a lemon, thinking is this a wind-up, why can't I get in? Coming down the road was a cyclist and he immediately pulled up and came over to me.

'Hello, are you Peter Ryder'?

'Why'? I said

'Because my name is Dave Apps, I started last week, nice to meet you, blimey your thin, you look like a *Bryant and May* reject.

'What?

'You know those matches that light fags' he kept going on. What an introduction. I took an immediate dislike to this Moron and then a gentleman came over and introduced himself as Jim Ryan the Orders manager. He unlocked the door and we all marched up three floors to the office. There wasn't much of a lift, so climbing the stairs we go! I don't know where he parked his bike and I sure didn't care.

I was also introduced to Mr Knox he was Dave Apps's mentor and then a Mr Twist who was going to be mine. We both got white coats to put on. I felt like an idiot, looked like a doctor but kept my thoughts to myself.

We were explained how the printing machine worked, make a cup of tea and answer the phone. Really exciting stuff............... go and get sandwiches and fags and that was about the extent of my first day at work.
Nine until five thirty and then the long trek home, arriving at 7.0pm.

Crikey is this how I am going to spend the rest of my life, not enjoying life but going to work and getting totally depressed about it. My mother asked me how it went and I said Awful. I hate it and I don't want to go back, but of course I did. It was that or the Dole. Even considered running away from home, but that had no future either. So I went to bed and got up again and again and again.......the future to me certainly didn't seem bright at this time.

Dave and I were told by our superiors to enrol at a college, locally to where we live. Dave was also a Dagenham boy. So we had a day off with pay. Yippy!

I went along to the South East Essex College in Dagenham and enrolled in a course for Builders and Engineers. The first year was for a City and Guilds course, mainly for tradesman with the following three years for professional engineers ONC (Ordinary National Certificate) course. I could easily get there by bus so that was ok. One day off a week plus two evenings a week and I was now on my way to forging a career. Just what my parents wanted of me – they were happy, but I wasn't.!!

The following day back at work my superiors asked me what day I was going to college and I said Wednesdays. Sorry son but Dave has that day so you will have to change it.

'I can't, it is the only day that this course can be attended' I said

'Well, you will just have to go to another college, we cannot have both of you out on the same day' moaned Mr Twist

'Why can't Dave change his college' I moaned back

'Because Dave signed up first' so that is why you will have to change yours. Now go back next week and try the East Ham Technical College and make sure it is a different day to Dave'

I thought bloody nuisance, trust him to get his way. However it eventually worked in my favour and I enrolled at that college on a different day to bloody Dave Apps.

I finally got a drawing to do from Mr Twist. It was a general arrangement of four flights of an external escape staircase to an office block. I had to draw on linen, in ink and get all my dimensions correct. It took me forever, especially with all my other tasks. Now I know what the white coat was for. For wiping the ink off on to my sleeve and stop it running all over the drawing.

That was a lesson learnt until Mr Twist said use a rag! Oh well, better late than never. My mother had to do the washing to get that damn white coat clean again.

My first weekly wage packet was given to me on Friday by Mr Shearer. He was a Jock and had a temper to match, another miserable bloke. I was rich nearly, £3.15.7p but my mother took some of that, I suppose it was now payback for all those years that I helped myself to that loose change out of her purse.

The weekend arrived, so I could now get to see *Rocky* and have some fun at last. What a week that was and there were hundreds more to come.

Chapter 20

College Begins

September arrived, and my first day at college. After the introductions to the lecturer I sat down in this Gloomy room and read the synopsis for the year ahead with about another thirty young men. They were all going to train to become plumbers, builders and carpenter's, I was the only one in the class that was apprenticed to be a draughtsman.

The subjects were Design engineering, strength of concrete, timber and brickwork. We spent the morning on one and the afternoon on another. Come back in the evening for another subject plus another evening for the last. This was hard work and most of us did not look forward to it. The daytime subjects were fine because we would have been at work anyway but the evenings were the worst. I never got home until about 9.30pm 'Knackered'. Then up in the morning for another day at the office.

I had to tackle a new way of calculating mathematical problems. This was really difficult. Calculators had not been invented then, so along came the slide rule. A sliding stick that could multiply, divides, subtract and add. It kind of was great as long as you knew where to put the decimal point! I had to buy this myself and it was bloody expensive. So now it was time to purchase tools of the trade and all out of my meagre weekly wage.

Some of the things we did were quite interesting. I remember we all had to make a cube of concrete from the cement and sand, wait fourteen to twenty one days and then put it under a machine that would eventually crush it. I thought Wow! That was good but what was the point. It did have a point, I was later to discover.

I was now beginning to enjoy my schooling and showing more of an interest in the subjects. It was early days but the beginning of a career that would eventually be rewarding.

The ABC cinema was about to close and something called a Bowling alley would open soon. Old 'Max Bygraves' sang a song about these changes. Fings aint wot they used to be', with one line that read,
'There changing our local Palais into a bowling alley, and fings aint wot they used to be'.
Always remembered this and how true it still is today.

Arthur was still my mate and at weekends we would still get in to see the local 'X' films at the ABC. They were not as frightening now so that was an improvement.
There was a notice put up outside the ABC stating that the cinema was closing down in a few weeks. We both thought, Oh no! What with the chequers closing down earlier in the year that would only leave the Heathway cinema open in our region. Everyone blamed the progress of television for this catastrophe; cinemas all over the country were closing down now with the advance of the bowling alleys taking over

I took to bowling, like a duck to water. Absolutely loved it, problem was it was damned expensive. I probably spent 30% of my weekly wages playing this sport.

Harry asked me, Arthur, Tommy, James and Freddie if we were interested in playing in the bowling league at the Princess Bowling Alley, as it was now called. We all jumped at the opportunity. The Metropolitan league was born, and every Tuesday night for about six months we played. Sometimes we even played away at Ilford or Streatham, but mostly it was at the Princess.

As strange as it may seem, we were crowned champions. The 'Demons' was our team name and this was the inauguration season 1960-61, the best team in the league and we were only sixteen years old. Everyone said we had a bright future, but to us this was a hobby and anyway we all had other interest at the time, so it was never gonna go that far. But Harry and I kept it up for a while and we were better than the average Joe.

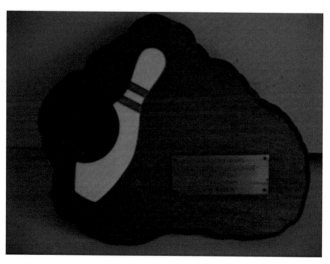

1960-61 Trophy

Chapter 21
Dance Revolution

A music craze had just started to hit the airwaves. *Chubby Checker* and 'The Twist' a dance that could be performed without a dancing partner So Arthur and I practiced it, but where to go and perform it was the problem. We soon found out that the East Ham Town Hall was open on Saturday nights and a live band performed there. Off we go, dance night and the start of many. We were both still shy lads and to dance with girls was still a 'no no'. But hey, we did have a great time.

This was the time of Elvis, Cliff, Adam Faith, Roy Orbison, Johnny Burnett, Bobby Vee, The Four Seasons, Bobby Darin and many more that I just loved to listen too. Who would have thought that the sixties would leave such an impression on me when I grew up?

Arthur and I thought that if we were going to hit it off with the girls then we would need to learn how to dance properly. Most dance venues were for serious dancing. The Waltz, Foxtrot and the rest of that serious stuff. The jive and dances for kids of our generation were popular, but there were few venues to strut our stuff. So we enrolled for dance lessons above Burtons at the Heathway.

On attendance at our first dance lesson we were met by a Mr Toms and his wife, who politely asked us to sit down around the side of the hall with loads of other potential dance partners.

'Arthur, what on earth are we doing here?' I whispered to him.

'I dunno really, everyone here is old enough to be our parents and they all tower above us,

I know we really have 'balls'ed' up here mate' I said.

Mr Toms and his wife started to perform a waltz to the music of a Sinatra standard, I think. Everyone in the room had to study this dance move for about five minutes. I remember these words. One, two three – one two three four and so on, this was the sequence of the steps that we all had to learn.

'OK ladies and gentleman please choose your partners for this dance' he shouted.

Mostly everyone got up from their seats, those who came with partners that is.

Arthur and I just sat glued to our chairs and just stared at each other.

Mr Toms disappeared and then suddenly reappeared with two massive Alsatian dogs. They came up to me and Arthur growling like rabid animals

.'Now get up you two and grab a partner to dance' he ranted this time.

So we did. Arthur's woman was much taller than him; his head was about level with her chest. I couldn't stop laughing...............Then I was approached by my dance partner, she was an old woman in her sixties. Arthur now started to laugh.

Needless to say, that was our first and last lesson. It was back to the '*Twist*' and '*hand jive*' from now on. Another lesson learnt, or mistake made, depending on how you looked at it!

Chapter 22

1961

I was really starting to enjoy my college work now, with interesting lessons, totally different from my schooldays, with more emphasis on practical as well as theory. This year was just a prelude to the more serious ONC which would start next term. I was a shining star in the lessons that we were all doing. The other lads' were budding plumbers and carpenters, but me, well I was to become a draughtsman and that was a great career in those days. For reasons I can't explain, but maybe my limited education was better than I even thought. I worked hard, did my homework and was getting good exam test results. The other lads were even starting to call me professor as a joke. I sometimes helped them with their homework and we all got along just fine.

Exam time was early May. I contracted a bad asthma attack at this time, which progressed to pneumonia. My build up for the exams was now useless. There was no way that I could recover to sit these exams. I was totally *gutted.* All that work for nothing or so I thought. As I previously mentioned, this year really had no bearing on the years to come. After all it was only a prelude and it was to give me great encouragement for the more serious exams commencing in 1962 for my National Diplomas. The boss at work gave me positive signs and said that the company will be giving me an apprenticeship. I did think that because I hadn't completed the exams that maybe just maybe they would terminate my employment. I needn't had worried, they supported me all the way.

I was now approaching the grand old age of sixteen. *Rocky* was still my mate and we would still see each other at the weekends and light summer evenings. But I was now getting interested in motor scooters. My parents didn't object and with my Pa we visited Albons in Barking, a scooter specialist. Pa chose this Lambretta for me. Did a test run, a mechanical check and hey presto I was a proud owner of 59 PNO (number plate). I purchased it with most of the money my Grandma gave me a few years back when Grandpa Baylis died. Actual cost was 105 pounds, so I still had some money left out of the £150.

I now had wheels and the freedom to travel anywhere, to work, college and beyond. No more stuffy trains, no schedule to worry about........fantastic.

No summer holidays this year. I got paid two weeks money and time off from work. I felt like a millionaire with all this money, but what did I do with it all? spent it down the bowling alley, every day. It didn't last long, but at least my scores were improving.

There was a midnight bowl at the alley during this period and it was quite popular. I turned up at about 10.0pm and they opened the lanes for about thirty minutes for everyone to practice. We played in teams of five as usual, selected by the alley manager. Prizes were up for grabs, so it was well worth winning, fags, booze and the compulsory cuddly toy. I achieved the highest score ever, that night with a score of 265 out of 300. I had eight strikes, five and then another three. Our team won, for the top score and of course I won the individual prize. Wow! And what did they give me, the booze............. I didn't drink in those days, so I gave it all away to a pal that did. What a waste, but it was a great night until *'crash'* the sound of breaking glass came from the entrance to the alley. A big drunken idiot came bounding up the main hallway with blood splattered all over him, shouting obscenities and ready to take the world on with his iron bar of a weapon. I recognised the hooligan; it was the kid, *Coote!* That was his name the one who took on the nice kid at school a couple of years ago. The bouncers quickly raced forward to intercept him, but not without a fight. All of us bowlers were watching from a safe distance and then the police turned up...................they took him away, thank goodness. It was about 2.0am and I was ready to go home. Exciting night out, that was for sure.

I was starting to earn extra money now because of my scooter. My boss at work was getting me to deliver drawings to *'WC Thompsons'* a fabricator situated under the flyover at Canning Town. Also collecting boxes of bolts from a supplier at Limehouse and delivering them to the sites. I used to charge three pence for every mile and when you think a gallon of petrol was 1/11p and I was getting 60 miles to the gallon, then the profit was quite rewarding. However all this had to be offset by the on-going expense of my scooter. Cable clutch breaking, servicing etc.

Arthur bought a scooter as well this year, a Vespa. It looked like a bumblebee with two big humps either side of the chassis. I always remember on one particular occasion we went to a pop concert at the Odeon East Ham, one wintry Saturday evening in November, to see Adam Faith, Eden Kane and a few other stars at that time. I don't know why we bothered really. The girls didn't stop screaming and shouting and we just could not hear our favourite songs.

With the concert finished we both headed back to the car park to collect our bikes. Kick started the engines and started to accelerate when Arthur fell off. I turned around; he and the bike were lying on the ground. His back wheel was missing. Someone had nicked his back wheel and propped the rear of the bike on bricks. We hadn't noticed this and unfortunately Arthur took a tumble. The bast..ds, we had to leave his bike there and I gave him a lift home. We collected the bike the next day. My Pa managed to put it in the boot of his car and Arthur had to pay out for a new wheel. Arthur worked in a factory (May and Bakers) near Dagenham East station and his wages were twice mine. I used to get a bit peeved off with this but Pa kept insisting that my job was a career and Arthur's was not and that the future would be more beneficial financially to me and not to give up.

On all future journeys on our bikes we now carried chain padlocks. No more wheels were stolen when parked, although looking back in hindsight I am surprised that the bike wasn't taken completely.

There was about eight of us now with scooters. So we all decided it might be a good idea to form a club and give ourselves a name. We came up with the name 'Confederates'. We were a proper team................ready to take on the world, or so we thought. Twice a week we would all meet up at the New road Inn, near the Chequers. A coffee house but with boarders who worked at Fords. We would play our favourite records on the Jukebox, drink coffee and make decisions for the weekend. This was our club and we all loved it.

Arthur was my real first mate. I would often go to his house prior to going out for the day or evening. His mum would always welcome me into her house and I would always have to wait for Arthur to get ready. His old man would come home from work, an unusual kind of guy really with some weird habits that I and Arthur would agree on. He would sit down in the front room and immediately demand his wife to bring him his dinner. Whereby he would scoff it down, washed down with his cup of tea. I remember on one occasion I was about to call for Arthur. But his sister was at the front door and their old man was hanging outside the front bedroom immediately above. 'Let me in Dad?' she was shouting up to him and with that, their old man threw a bucket of water over her. I thought what an idiot why did he have to do that.

When Arthur came out the front door he explained to me that their parents had an awful argument and it was about his sister going out with a boy. Apparently she was banned to even talk to boys let alone go out with one. He was completely 'off his rockers'. Their mother and Arthur tried to keep it a secret because they knew how he would react if he found out.

Then one day something really awful happened.................it was devastating not just to the family but the whole street was effected by this piece of bad news. Their mother had come home from shopping one early afternoon, entered the front door, walked through to the kitchen and screamed!

Arthur's Dad had hung himself from the landing upstairs. Nobody really understood why, but Arthur himself thought he was a really depressed man and there was obviously some demons playing in his mind – just devastating this whole episode

On the August bank holiday weekend we all decided to have a trip to Walton-On-The-Naze and camp out for the night. But first I had to go to the 'Army and Navy' surplus shop in East Ham to purchase my ex-army over coat. These were all the rage. This coat looked like a bear's skin and came down to your knees. It was ideal for the road trips. Apparently the army chaps used to wear them in Norway for manoeuvre's in the snow, so this was a must wear item.

We all set out on the Sunday, but when we arrived, there was so many people at Walton and all the campsites were full. Also they would not allow us noisy scooter gangs to camp overnight, bloody typical, just when you want to enjoy yourself there was always someone or somebody to spoil it. We blame the media for this. They called us 'Mods'. Gangs with motorbikes were called 'Rockers'. Anyway we moved on to a car park within a mile of the seafront and started to unpack our bags to put up our tents, when approaching us from the road, a couple of 'Coppers', (Policeman).

'What do you think you lot are doing here' he shouted. James answered him back.

'What does it look like Constable' with the emphasis on the cont......'we are about to camp for the night' he politely commented. Whack! He hit James around his right ear and shouted to all of us to move on.

'You can't do that' James shouted

'Oh yes we can, now move on and get out of here, far away or you will all be coming down to the station to spend the night in a cell.'

So we moved on, drove all the way back home. What a bloody mess, as soon as you have a group of two or more, you are classified as an undesirable.

The following day on the news, Bank holiday Monday, news was coming in on the TV of gangs of Mods and Rockers fighting in the towns and on the beaches. Overturning side stalls, fighting the Police and even attacking holiday makers. This was happening all over the country at most seaside towns. So that was the reason for the Police to move us on. It was like an epidemic and it would always happen at holiday periods. Obviously the Confederates were not that kind of gang. But we obviously got brought in to this by association. From now on when we had days out, the seaside was out of bounds.

I came out of my house one day, got on the scooter and could see all the other lads at the end of the road. With another one of my stupid ideas I thought I would scare them. I raced down the road and thought I would make out that I was going to crash in to them. Brake suddenly and have a laugh.

Well! That didn't quite work out. I scared them alright. I braked but I didn't stop. My scooter hit the ground on its side with me saddled across it. I careered as if in slow motion with gasp of fear coming from the faces of all my mates.

Crash!.................. it was over in seconds. One by one I seemed to hit them. Like a bowling ball getting a strike at the bowling alley. Oh jeeze what have I done this time? I thought to myself this is really bad. The scooters and mates were all over the road and everyone were now shouting at me. Cuts and bruises were admonished to everyone, no one escaped. My own scooter came

147 Red

out with the least damage protected by my crash bars. My arms and knees were cut but fortunately not serious.

James was the first to speak 'you bloody idiot Ginge, what did you think you were doing?' he shouted.

I didn't mean it' I sheepishly explained 'It was an accident'

It was all sorted, no one was really injured and all the bikes just had a few scratches. All was forgiven thankfully so off we went for another adventure.

Arthur and I still continued to try dancing. We would get on our bikes and drive to the Ilford Palais, Tottenham Royal and to Basildon at the Locarno. But as usual, never asked the girls for a dance. All these venues had live Orchestra's and we really enjoyed the music, it was a great night out. One venue that we frequented a lot was Victor Silvester's in Romford. We would catch a bus there and pay the admittance price. Inside as usual was the band, only difference with this venue you could purchase another ticket and enter the disco upstairs. For one hour only the music of Cliff, Adam, the Big O, Elvis and so on. When the hour was up another bunch of kids would come in and we had to return to the dance floor. The only disco in town!!

We would still go to the live shows. At the Walthamstow Gaumont, Del Shannon, The Big O and Brenda Lee were all appearing for one night only. This was a must and a great night out once again

September arrived again and the beginning of the first year of my college studies. I was now attending college again. This would be one day a week plus two evenings. The object was to achieve my ONC in Building, a three year course followed by a two year course for my HNC. When you are only 16 years of age and venturing to spend five years to achieve academic qualifications, it can seem like a lifetime and that is exactly how it felt. I always remember my brother trying to achieve these goals in electrical engineering and failing. He still achieved good employment. He was in my opinion at the time a very bright person, although a bit dim on dealing with me as a kid.

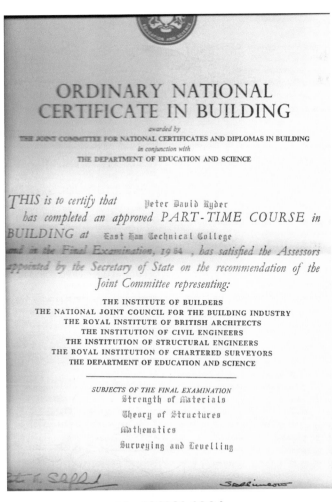

My 'ONC' 1964

Towards Christmas my company were organising a 'Do' for the eight employees. It was held in a restaurant in the West End. This was a first for me and quite daunting really. I had to buy a suit, a new shirt, didn't want Dave Apps to get one over me. I felt like a fish out of water. Everyone knew the etiquette of dining, but not me. I didn't know what utensil to use, what glass and so on.....................neither did Dave, so I wasn't alone. He had such a big mouth. The times I wanted to plant one on him, were just immense, but I didn't of course. Had my first alcoholic drink, a light ale in a bottle. It was horrible. Put me off having another one for quite some time. However I did enjoy myself and looked forward to the next time.

In my pay packet every week was 10 shillings of Luncheon vouchers. They were absolutely useless to me or so I thought. You could not cash them in because one had to spend them on lunches or sandwiches and I always brought sandwiches to work, made lovingly by my Mother. They were always 'cheese and pickle' I never had anything else. These vouchers contributed to about 13% of my wages and that was a lot. Anyway a friend of a friend said to me. If I went to a café close to the 'Old Bailey' called 'Piccolinos' he would exchange them for packets of fags. I thought really! So I would save about one month's worth and trot along to the café and buy a few packets. I personally didn't really smoke them, but I knew people who did and of course Maggi liked 'Kensitas' fags so I use to do a deal with her and some of my mates. Some habits just don't die!! But I couldn't believe that right opposite the Queens Court of

Justice that you could get away with this. It probably wasn't a criminal offence, but it certainly felt like it.

On one particular day my scooter had to go in for repairs at Albons. I therefore went to work on the trains again. Thinking to myself, why pay I'll just walk through the barrier at my destination, no problems there, or so I thought.

However on this day in mention the Central line had been suspended so I kept on the District line train through to the Embankment. I could easily walk to Furnival Street from there. As I approached the end of the escalator I could see the 'Gestapo Squad' (ticket inspectors) at the gates checking every passenger's tickets. They obviously pulled me aside and cross examined me. I tried to blag myself out of trouble but as usual in these cases just got into more trouble. They told me to expect a summons in the post and that I would be prosecuted. I would have to go to court and expect the worst. That certainly scared the sh.t out of me. For three months I had the worry of what would they do to me. Would I go to jail, probation or just a fine?

Obviously I didn't tell anyone. Not my parents and definitely not my company

The Magistrates court at Mansion House was where I had to attend. I had to sit in the gallery upstairs and wait for the court to call me. 'Harold Peter Ryder' finally was shouted, but I ignored this. I thought what a coincident someone with part of my name here as well. They called that name again and then one of the court officers shouted at me 'that's you son, go down in front of the magistrate now'. What an idiot, it wasn't Harold it was heralding................Peter Ryder.

Oh well! I discovered something else that day, that's for sure.

I was fined ten pounds with costs of five pounds. This was a lot of money for me to find. I had four weeks to get it, nearly one month's wages. Had to raid my little pot of savings and just carry on. A lesson learnt.

Chapter 23
1962- Part 1

Near the end of my early years.

I was presented with a Scooter Diary for one of my Christmas presents. But I didn't religiously keep records, just moments recalled over the year. I was now interested in maths and average figures and so on……

For the first three months I would write down my petrol consumption, mileage and price. What an earth for I'm not sure, Probably to keep records just to make it interesting for me……………never ever thought I would still have this diary today. So to keep the record straight I have added a few pages into this chapter, boring I know……….

I was now doing regular runs for 'Ellis Jones' on my scooter and this was welcomed additional revenue for me. I would still collect packages of bolts and deliver them to the Steel Erectors on various sites all over London. On one particular visit I had to go to a sewage works in north London. The Supervisor showed me around and kind of tried to educate me on the workings of the sewage works. I thought it was quite interesting but SMELLY! The next stop was over to west London, where a factory warehouse was being erected. This was part of a project that I had actually completed some drawings on. So I was fascinated by this experience. On the way back to the office I popped in to a café for a cup of tea, got back to my scooter and adjusted the remainder of bolts that were in my steel carrier at the rear of the scooter. When suddenly the spring which held the bolts broke and it sprung back and spliced right through my finger. 'Owch!................that hurt'. The spring had cut right through and once again blood was everywhere. For once I didn't faint. I wrapped it up as quickly as I could with a piece of rag from my toolbox and rushed to the A and E, which was just around the corner. With a small injection and a few stiches I was on my way again. Phew! That was lucky. When I got back to the office my boss could still see I was shaken by the experience so he let me go home early. That was a result, home early for a change, on this horrible January day.

My brother bought all his suits made to measure from 'Lew Rose' a bespoke tailor's at East Ham High Street. If it was good enough for him then it was good enough for me, even though I couldn't really afford one at this time. I would go along to the tailors get made to measure for my first suit.

'A Blue Teutonic, Italian style'. How chuffed I felt. I paid the tailor a small deposit and had to return twice for a fitting. He said it would be ready in about six weeks, so that gave me time to save for the suit. It cost me about £12, three times my salary so I started saving 10 shillings a week. I know that wasn't enough, but with my scooter travel money from work I was sure it would be OK.

My scooter was now starting to cost me more in upkeep. I had to get the carrier repaired for welding, after that little episode with my finger. The carrier was broken so I took it to a welding shop in Rainham to be fixed, cost 3 shillings. Then my clutch cable broke 1/6p. Back light bulb went 2/9d, followed by the throttle cable £1-5-10d this was expensive. Had to have it repaired in London while at work. I just couldn't believe this. Now my front brake cable needed to be replaced 3/9d.

Is this ever going to stop? I thought at this rate I might as well go back to work on the trains, It could be less expensive.

Pa asked me if I would like to go on holiday in June to Jersey. I jumped at it thinking he would pay. But was I disappointed! He said I had to save for it myself and that he would help out if I was short. What a tight b*****d I thought to myself. Ma didn't want to go, so I was his next option. I now had to save £1 per week and give it to him.

What with my scooter breakdowns, saving for a suit, court fines and finally saving for my holidays. Times were getting hard. Its' fortunate my brother now believed in Banks, otherwise I might have been tempted to rob his money cigar box again................

I travelled 100 miles this month on my scooter for Ellis-Jones at 3d per mile, so my total reward worked out at £3 and that was most welcome to help my finances.

Sunday nights were now reserved for bowling. Harry and I would have a game to practice for the league nights, but my highest score was only 144 this time and this turned out to be my average score for quite some time.

I keep telling myself to spend less money, but it is hard. You're only young once and I seemed to think money was still grown on trees.

This week Arthur and I went to the Cinema twice. A Frank Sinatra film called 'The Devil at 4 o/c' and 'Revak the Rebel'. Well! It was winter and it kept us out of trouble. No dancing at the Palais this week. Cinema was the cheaper option.

It's the beginning of February and I have now saved £4-15-0 towards my suit. Going well I thought. Then on Sunday another film 'Splendour in the Grass' what a load of rubbish that was. Arthur and I only went because it was an X film.

This month I have managed 120 miles for Ellis-Jones, a good month, with a payment of £3-5-0d saved, £5 towards my suit and paid Pa £6-5-0 for my holidays. I'm thinking to myself, should have trained to be an accountant and not this draughtsman stuff. That profession might have paid me more.

My complete gear cable broke and I had to take it in to Albons to get it replaced. What a rip off!..................that little item cost me £1-5-0.

On March the 6th I was recruited to join up with a new bowling team called the 'HAWKS'. Four old men and me. They were actually sponsored by a brewery. I think it was called the Double Diamond, Trueman Brewery, but not really sure. I didn't do too well on my first game and only scored 124,117,108. They were all right about my low scores and said it was probably nerves. Just as well, not that I was really bothered, anyway. The following week was much improved, 156,125,160.

This scooter of mine has now developed a broken exhaust. So it's back to the welders to fix, certainly, not paying out for a new one, not yet anyway. But it still cost me 12/6.

Arthur and I drove to Clacton on Sunday 26th for the day. 130 miles return, really enjoyed it. Had a walk along the beach, fish and chips plus an ice cream, what a great day. My Bowling score improved again on Tuesday, 183,178,154 so the Hawks were really pleased as we started to march up the league. On Sunday 1st April a group of us drove to Dymchurch Hastings, for the day. 180 miles return. Pa didn't get his £1 this week couldn't afford it; my plan was now starting to work.

Harry and I had a chat about saving money by sharing our Scooters for travelling to work. We would do alternate days', I still needed cash from work if needed be.

So on Monday 9th April it was on. Harry used his bike first and I was the pinion passenger. This little arrangement worked fine and we continued it for quite some months, until one wet and windy day driving home from work we nearly had an accident. Harry in his wisdom had decided to overtake this enormous lorry on the A13 at the Becton by pass. From the opposite direction another huge lorry was approaching. The rain was pelting down and the cross wind was certainly strong,

'Harry pull out?' I shouted, but not Harry. Onwards and forwards he continued. I could see that the gap between the two Lorries' was miniscule and thought I would die that day under the wheels of two six ton trucks. I closed my eyes and crossed my fingers. Whoosh!................... The scooter was caught in the downdraft as the two Lorries passed each other, we were barracked from side to side, it seemed like an eternity until we made it, and eventually passed in front of the lorry, safely through continuing with our journey. I really shouted at 'Harry boy' and said that's it, never again. If I'm going to die on the road then it will be down to me and not some other person. I guess Harry did well manoeuvring us through that chicane, but of course I never told him that at the time.

Early spring and Harry and I were having a chat with a couple of girls down our road. Not sure of their names now, but they thought it would be a good idea if Harry and I gave them a lift on the back of our scooters to work the next day. They both worked in an office in London. So obviously we said yes! Only one small detail Girls I explained. We have not passed our tests yet and therefore we would be breaking the law. 'So what' said Helen, I think that was her name? 'OK' if you're up for it, then so are we'. Picked them up in the morning and off we went to London in the rush hour as per normal.

Why does it always happen to me? Harry was away and I was close on his tails. We were approaching the traffic lights at the end of the Beckton bypass when the lights changed from green to red. Harry missed the red and carried on. I pulled up as you would expect, close to the kerb. However a lorry travelling to fast decided he was not going to stop. Guess what? The lorry clipped my scooter kick start pedal and that immediately turned my bike around, we both came off, crashing to the ground. I was completely dazed and Helen was screaming. Pedestrians waiting to cross all came over to help us. 'Bloody idiot that lorry driver' an elderly woman shouted as she and her friend helped me and Helen up. 'I have his number son' she said. But Helen was in a worst condition than me. Her leg was broken. The Ambulance arrived and I was so sorry for her. But the Police didn't. She said 'don't worry I won't report the accident Pete'. She was true to her word. The police never appeared and I was on my way again. I saw her a few days later with her leg in plaster. She was really good about the accident, even her mother never knew the real truth on what had happened, thank goodness. Oh! And miraculously my bike was undamaged.

I passed my test early spring, so at least now pinion riders and me were legal.

I had a crash helmet that was totally white in colour. I would paint characters of 'Micky Mouse', 'Donald Duck' and Rocky on the helmet. I mention this because it got stolen. My scooter was always parked during the day when I was at work on the central reservation in the road opposite Gamages, departmental store and Leather Lane. This one particular late afternoon after leaving work, someone had 'half inched it' (pinched it). I therefore had to drive home without my favourite helmet. It wasn't illegal at the time, so that wasn't a problem, but it did have great sentimental value to me. Anyway a couple of days later during my lunchtime I was strolling down Leather lane and saw my helmet on a sellers stall. So I said to this guy 'hey Mister that is my crash helmet that you have there and I want it back'.

'Cost you 10 shillings lad if you want it'.

'But it's mine; it was stolen from my bike',

'Sonny I don't care if it was stolen from the Queen herself, it will still cost you 10 shillings',

'I'll call the Police' - I shouted back to him, thinking that would embarrass him to give it to me, especially with so many people watching this little altercation.

'Look just p**s off, if you don't have proof of purchase, then you will just have to pay me the 10 shillings, now go away'

My last bit of bravados was to say I will, but I didn't and I was extremely upset. Nothing I could really do. Bought a second hand one for half the price at some local scooter shop, in the end.

Friday 20th April the Easter weekend. Arthur, James and me had decided we would go camping. The destination was the Forest of Dean Monmouthshire. Why there? I don't know really but it seemed like a good idea at the time. We had a couple of tents, packed our sleeping bags, saucepan, plates, cup, knife and fork and toothbrush. Spare shirt, trousers and we were ready for the trip, over 350 miles return.

We arrived safe and sound on our bikes, pitched the tents and went to the camp coffee shop for a bite to eat and drink. Still didn't drink alcohol. Arthur went to his tent and James and I slept in mine. But not for long. The heavens opened up, it was a torrential downpour. The wind picked up and we had to hold on to the tent poles. We had pitched the tents on the side of a hill, bloody idiots, nobody warned us about this stupid error. The rain just kept falling; it was running down the hill like a bloody river and washing us away. Arthur's tent disappeared over the horizon and he came in to ours, for what good that did us all. But we did manage to hold on to it. Didn't get any sleep, soaking wet and totally p*****d off. When daylight arrived we rang out our clothes and biked sorrowfully to the nearest place that was open. A garage about ten minutes away. It was 7.0 am; we walked in to the shop, had a hot cup of tea and moaned about our night to the proprietor. He started to cheer us up surprisingly. 'Boys' he said 'stick it out for another night, for tomorrow will be fantastic. Hot and sunny'

'How do you know?' I moaned, 'just take it from me, I'm never wrong'

You know what? He was 100% correct and Sunday was brilliant, a bloody heat wave, we had a great time. Cooked our bacon and eggs in the morning and explored the Forest of Dean, such a beautiful place. We all returned home on Monday.

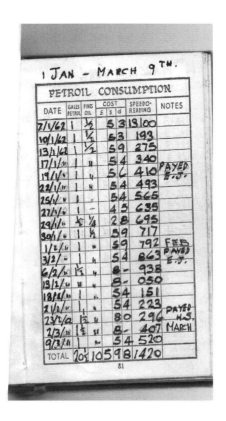

PETROIL CONSUMPTION

DATE	GALLS PETROL	PINTS OIL	COST £	s	d	SPEEDO-READING	NOTES
7/1/62	1	½		5	3	18100	
10/1/62	1	½		53		193	
13/1/62	1	½		59		275	
17/1/"	1	"		54		340	
19/1/"	1	"		56		410	PAYED E.J.
22/1/"	1	"		54		493	
25/1/"	1			54		565	
27/1/"	1	-		45		635	
29/1/"	½	¼		28		695	
30/1/"	1	½		59		717	
1/2/"	1	"		59		792	FEB PAYED E.J.
3/2/"	1	"		54		863	
6/2/"	1½	"		8	-	938	
13/2/"	"	"		8	-	050	
18/2/"	1	"		54		151	
21/2/"	1	"		54		223	
23/2/2	1½	"		80		296	PAYED H.S.
2/3/"	1½	"		8	-	407	MARCH
9/3/"	1	"		54		520	
TOTAL	20	10	5	9	8	1420	

81

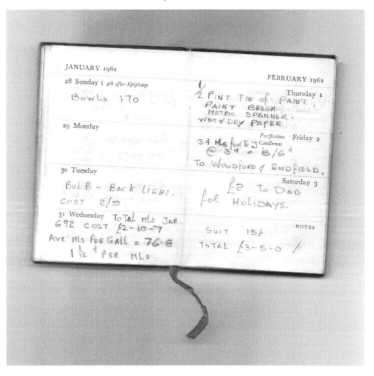

Diary Extracts

More 'Boring' Diary Extracts

162 Red

Part 2

It is now getting towards the end of my first year at college ONC class. Now preparing for the first of four tests this year, strength of materials, theory of structures, Maths and surveying and levelling. Maths was my Achilles heel. I was useless at this subject. But I did excel at the rest, so that was something to be positive about I suppose, especially theory of structures, I did find this subject interesting and would obtain a distinction in my final years of the HNC course 1966. A couple of 1962 college samples I have included, just to complete the picture

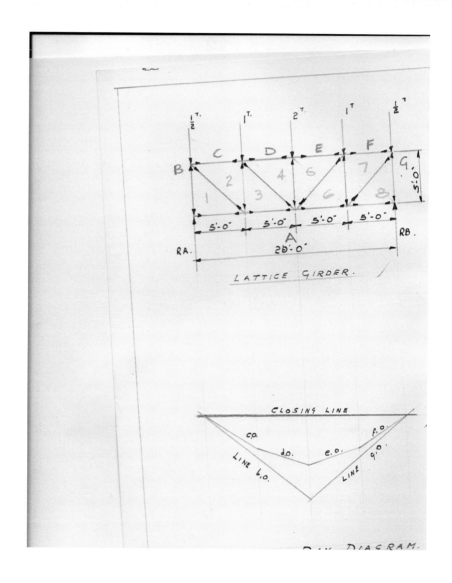

LATTICE GIRDER.

CLOSING LINE

DIAGRAM.

164 Red

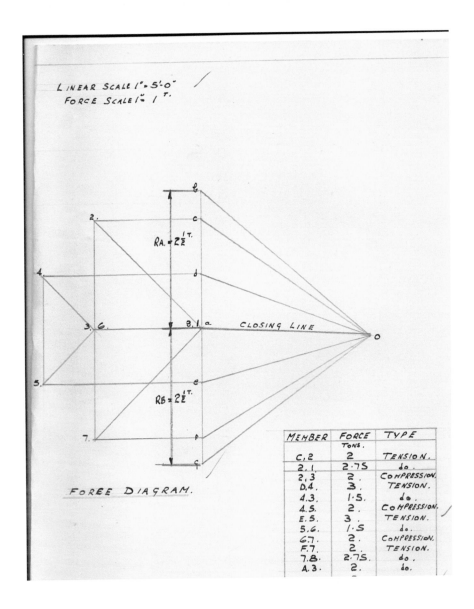

LINEAR SCALE 1" = 5'-0"
FORCE SCALE 1" = 1 T.

$RA. = 2\frac{1}{2}$ T.

CLOSING LINE

$RB = 2\frac{1}{2}$ T.

FORCE DIAGRAM.

MEMBER	FORCE TONS.	TYPE
C, 2	2	TENSION.
2. 1.	2.75	do.
2, 3	2.	COMPRESSION.
D. 4.	3.	TENSION.
4. 3.	1.5.	do.
4. 5.	2.	COMPRESSION.
E. 5.	3.	TENSION.
5. 6.	1.5	do..
6. 7.	2.	COMPRESSION.
F. 7.	2.	TENSION.
7. 8.	2.75.	do.
A. 3.	2.	do.

The music charts were fantastic this year. A song came out by an American country singer called Marty Robbins 'Devil Woman' was the title. I absolutely loved this record and I knew Maggi did as well, so with her birthday on the horizon 20th May I bought it for her. She thought it was great, strange how I remember this particular moment in time.

165 Red

The hits kept on rolling, what a glorious year.

Frank Ifield	I Remember You
Mr Acker Bilk	Stranger On The Shore
The Tornados	Telstar
Elvis Presley	Good Luck Charm
Chubby Checker	Let's Twist Again
Frank Ifield	Lovesick Blues
Mike Sarne With Wendy Richard	Come Outside
Joe Brown	A Picture Of You
Pat Boone	Speedy Gonzales
Cliff Richard	Do You Want To Dance / I'm Looking Out The Window
Elvis Presley	She's Not You
Helen Shapiro	Tell Me What He Said
Little Eva	The Loco-Motion
Bobby Darin	Things
Roy Orbison	Dream Baby
Del Shannon	Swiss Maid
Karl Denver	Wimoweh
Del Shannon	Hey Little Girl
Elvis Presley	Return To Sender
Eden Kane	Forget Me Not
Brian Hyland	Ginny Come Lately
Susan Maughan	Bobby's Girl
Tommy Roe	Sheila
Leroy Van Dyke	Walk On By
Bruce Channel	Hey Baby
Billy Fury	Last Night Was Made For Love
Carole King	It Might As Well Rain Until September
Mark Wynter	Venus In Blue Jeans

Adam Faith	As You Like It
Neil Sedaka	Breaking Up Is Hard To Do
Rolf Harris	Sun Arise
Nat 'King' Cole	Ramblin' Rose
Bobby Vee	Run To Him
Kenny Ball & His Jazzmen	Midnight In Moscow
Sam Cooke	Twistin' The Night Away
Matt Monro	Softly, As I Leave You

I have now paid Pa £14 towards my holiday with him. No more, that's it, he let me off the final payments and on Friday 22nd June we were off to Jersey 'Pontins' holiday camp. Travelled to Southend airport, Pa drove in his Ford Anglia and parked it at the airport. A prop jet flew us to Jersey, a 45 minute flight without any hic-cups. That certainly made a change from the last time I was here about six years ago. A bus picked us up from Jersey airport when we arrived, for our final destination 'Plemont Bay'. Shared a cabin with Pa, that was alright, I suppose.

Plemont Bay was on a hilltop, and there must have been about two thousand steps to walk down to get to the beach. Alright going down, but UP........forget it. I did this once and never again. Stayed by the pool during the day and entered all those silly competitions for snooker, table tennis, darts and anything else that was going on at the time. I don't know what Pa was up to, probably propping up the bar all day. I never won any of those competitions, what a pity there wasn't a bowling alley!

The evenings were spent in the ballroom, watching the bad acts that performed every night. I would go to bed early and Pa would stagger in about midnight.

On one particular day Pa hired a car and we travelled around the Island to see the sights. But as usual nothing ever goes to plan. He hit the side of a bus and continued on driving.
I said ' aren't you going to stop?
'Wasn't my fault' he said, 'the steering on this car is useless'
'Yeh! well, maybe it was you and not the steering' but he wouldn't have it, so I don't know what the final outcome was and he never told me.

All and all I had a great time. It was time to go back home again after a week with some fine weather for a change.

Arthur and I were still mates and we did a trip to Southend again, just the two of us. Had our jellied eels and cockles, walked along the promenade and generally kept ourselves to ourselves, no trouble this time.
I was now helping out Mr Twist a lot, my immediate supervisor at work. We would venture out and conduct surveys of buildings that would require extensions. I would hold the tape at one end, not exactly exciting work, but at least I was out of the office for a few hours. The theodolite would be used to measure the datum levels and so on to get the correct measurements. This part was interesting. Once back in the office I would have to prepare the drawings for submission to the various clients.

One of the old boys in the office, a draughtsman, said to me 'Peter you should get out of this structural steel profession and go for the reinforced concrete design side of the industry. Steel is dead; concrete is going to be the new industry building material'. I said 'really' but took no notice of him. How wrong could he be? In the 1970's the Off-shore industry was born with the push for gas and oil in the North Sea and all though it was a struggle at first with very few opportunities it proved to be the most lucrative and long term employment for the rest of my life with work locations all over the globe.

I would always nag my mother about getting a dog. Over the years she would never listen. In the end I was quite happy with the Blackie and Rocky dog pals I had made. Then one day I get home from work and a friend of my mother's has given her a dog. A *'Bloody Poodle!!*. Of all the dogs she could choose, she chooses a *mad* poodle. Called it *Pepe* and it was really crazy. I took a dislike to it immediately. It would yap, run around like a headless chicken, you name it and that dog would be it.

I had rented an expensive technical book from my college library and while at work one day this mad dog had got hold of it and ripped chapters 12 to 15 to shreds I was not a happy bunny.....I tried to sneak this book back to the library without the librarian noticing. It wasn't to be; she fined me 8 shillings for the book and then told me to keep it. It now props up my computer. But that bloody dog really did grate on me.

The summer was coming to an end and Arthur and I would still be visiting the dance halls. We were at Romford again at Victor

Silvesters. A life changing moment, was about to happen this day in October.

'You ask first, I said to Arthur, 'Ok I will he replied'

'Girls! Do you wanna dance? my name is Arthur and this is Peter'

And to my surprize they said yes. So off we both trotted with our dance partners on to the dance floor, dancing to the latest sounds from the swing music of the day. A waltz, close up and smooth...............I thought this was fantastic, my first real dance with a beautiful girl. After the dance we asked them their name. 'My name is Pat' said Arthur's girl and my name is 'BRENDA', said my girl, 'we are Sisters'

Arthur eventually broke up with Pat, but I had another date with Brenda. We actually went to the cinema in Romford to see the smash hit 'Dr No' James Bond.

So that was the start of a new beginning, my wife to be three years later 1965

The rest is history and that is where I finish

171 Red

THE END

Author's Note

I guess this is the part where I say thank you to everyone who contributed to my story – but I can't think of anybody!................just joking.........

Thank you to my Wife (Brenda) for putting up with me.
Paul and Jayne (my kids) for bringing such joy and fulfilment to my life. I am so proud of them both – there I've said it, they probably never thought I would.

Thank you to all the kids, knowingly or not who participated in the recollection of memories for my book.
The reader for understanding, that this is an amateur writing and not a professional. There were spelling mistakes and bad Grammar in this book even with the spell check, mistakes are surely there.

It was only my intention to write my story for my lovely grandchildren, so that they would have a lasting memory of their Grandfather.

The End of the Beginning